A Passion for Difference

A Passion for Difference

Essays in Anthropology and Gender

HENRIETTA L. MOORE

Indiana University Press
Bloomington and Indianapolis

First published in North America in 1994 by Indiana University Press,
601 North Morton Street, Bloomington, Indiana, in association with Polity
Press, 65 Bridge Street, Cambridge CB2 1UR, UK.

Manufactured in Great Britain.

ISBN 0–253–20951–X paper
ISBN 0–253–33858–1 cloth

A CIP catalog record for this book is available from the Library of Congress.

*In memory
of
my mother
Josephine Moore
(1934–1993)*

CONTENTS

ACKNOWLEDGEMENTS

This book was produced during a period of leave from the London School of Economics made possible by a grant from the Leverhulme Trust. The Trust generously funded a project on 'The Development of Models for the Analysis of Gender in the Social Sciences' from 1 January to 31 December 1993. I am indebted to both institutions for their help and financial support.

Chapter 1 was originally published in *Feminist Review*, vol. 47, 1994, as 'Divided we stand: sex, gender and sexuality'.

Chapter 2 is a revised version of an article originally published as 'Gendered persons: dialogues between anthropology and psychoanalysis' in Suzette Heald and Ariane Deluz (eds), *Anthropology and Psychoanalysis: An Encounter through Culture*, London: Routledge, 1994.

Parts of chapter 3 originally appeared in 'The problem of explaining violence in the social sciences' in Peter Gow and Penelope Harvey (eds), *Sex and Violence: Issues in Representation and Experience*, London: Routledge, 1994.

Chapter 5 is a substantially revised version of an article originally published as 'Gender and the modelling of the economy' in Sutti Ortiz and Susan Lees (eds), *Understanding Economic Process*, Lanham: University Press of America, 1993.

Chapter 6 was originally published in Maurice Biriotti and Nicola Miller (eds), *What is an Author?*, Manchester: Manchester University Press, 1993.

I am very grateful to Routledge, Manchester University Press, the University Press of America and *Feminist Review* for permission to republish the above materials.

I have benefited enormously from the help and support of many friends and colleagues whilst writing these essays. I would particularly like to thank Michelle Stanworth, Marilyn Strathern and Megan Vaughan for their intellectual companionship, and for their criticisms which they always manage to couch in the most generous possible terms.

INTRODUCTION

A Passion for Difference

Difference exerts an uncanny fascination for all of us. Contemporary social and cultural theory exhibits an obsessive concern with issues of difference, and such is the malleability of the term that almost anything can be subsumed under it.[1] This passion for difference seems to be linked to its unspoken and under-theorized pair, 'the same' or 'sameness'. This is not implied, of course, in the deconstructionist notion of *différance*, but it is implicitly there in much feminist and social science theorizing, as well as in contemporary political activism. Deciding on differences is one way of delineating identities. Difference(s) from others are frequently about forming and maintaining group boundaries. The brutal and bloody nature of this maintenance work is everywhere in evidence.

Thinking about difference entails, then, thinking about identity and/or sameness. However, these latter terms are not themselves identical. Within the academy, establishing an understanding of the relations between difference and identity has been a complex and sometimes explosive task. Feminist scholars, in particular, have been struggling with the question of how or to what degree women might be the same or similar without being identical. What is it, if anything, that we share? This book is concerned with questions of difference, sameness and sharing. It also addresses the various rhetorical forms of 'we' at work in feminist and anthropological writing. Who or what does 'we' refer to in the contemporary moment? Problems of reference here are connected to issues of belonging.

Identity and difference are not so much about categorical groupings as about processes of identification and differentiation. These processes are engaged for all of us, in different ways, with the desire to belong, to be part of some community, however provisional. Belonging invokes desire, and it is in this desire that much of the passion for difference resides.

In terms of my own writing the question of where and to what I belong involves, as it does for others, a consideration of position and location. If I belong somewhere, then I speak and write from there, and the specifics of that location matter. But all locations are provisional, held in abeyance. One is never truly anywhere and if locations or positions are to be specified, they will always be in the plural. The crisis of location is a productive, but personally terrifying one. Both the label 'anthropologist' and that of 'feminist' remain under radical interrogation, and as a feminist anthropologist I find my relations with these terms to be strenuous, nuanced and unrelentingly complex. However, I am passionately committed, and this is what provides the energy and the propulsion for my work. The essays in this collection represent my attempts to come to grips with the questions of difference and sameness that being a feminist and an anthropologist raise.

Bodies and identities

The provisionality of positions reminds us that when we consider questions of location we are not simply trying to reinscribe an essentialism of place. Positionality is too often reduced to individual experience and/or to representation: 'I know because I've been there' and 'I know because I am one'. These slippages are particularly troublesome when linked to grounds for authority. Anthropology and feminism share a tendency to assert that experience acts as an ontological given. This issue has been discussed in many times and places, but what worries me here is the way in which experience is sometimes reduced to its linguistic and cognitive elements, to what I know and to what I can talk about. This process of reduction encourages a view of experience which sees it as ontological, singular and fixed. Experience can and does act ontologically for all of us, but it does so through a technique of construction. This process of construction involves a recognition of the role of physical presence in establishing dialogue between individuals and groups. What is at issue is the embodied nature of identities and experience. In subsequent chapters I propose a notion of the 'lived anatomy' and of bodily praxis as a mode of knowledge that draws on an understanding of experience as a form of embodied intersubjectivity. The very fact of being present as an embodied subject gives a particular character to the ontology of experience which emphasizes the degree to which social interactions are embodied ones taking place in concrete space and time.

Intersubjectivity and dialogue involve situations where bodies marked through by the social, that is, by difference (race, gender, ethnicity and so on), are presented as part of identities. The uses of the body, the particular circumstances of interaction and the readings made by others are all involved in the taking up of a position or positions that form the basis for the enunciation of experience. Experience is thus intersubjective and embodied; it is not individual and fixed, but irredeemably social and processual.

The experience of being a woman or being black or being a Muslim can never be a singular one, and will always be dependent on a multiplicity of locations and positions that are constructed socially, that is, intersubjectively. The intersubjectivity of experience is not confined, of course, to physical appearances, to actual dialogue and to the concrete nature of sociological circumstance. Intersubjectivity is also about identifications and recognitions. It is about desire and the projection and introjection of images of self and others. One of the major questions here, addressed in chapter 3 through issues concerning sexuality and violence, is the problem of how we construct and acquire identities, and how well these processes are captured by current theories in the social sciences.

The individual and the social

One of the major themes running through this book concerns the relationship between anthropology and psychoanalysis. I take anthropology to task in several ways for its failure to theorize the acquisition of gender identity and the multiple nature of subjectivity. One puzzling feature of the development of feminist anthropology has been its relative neglect of the debate concerning the deconstruction of the humanist subject. Chapter 2 suggests various ways in which cross-cultural data might be used to illuminate and contribute to feminist theorizing in this area.

My discussions of gender identity and gendered subjectivity work over a series of old, but unresolved themes about the relationship of the individual to the social and vice versa. Anthropology's emphasis on the social at the expense of the individual accounts in large part for its failure to develop a theory of the subject. However, the problem raised by cultural difference and its relation to gender difference is one about how processes of identification and recognition work. What makes the cultural discourses of gender powerful and how well do they regulate/constitute/represent people's experience of gender in any given context?

Post-structuralist theories of the subject and of positionality are useful here because they create a space in which it is possible to talk about the different subject positions proffered by various discourses. Thus, gendered subjectivity does not have to be conceived of as a fixed and singular identity, but can be seen instead as one based on a series of subject positions, some conflicting or mutually contradictory, that are offered by different discourses. This would be all very well were it not for the problem of how to account for the fact that individuals do not always take up the subject positions offered to them. One obvious point is that the existing discourses on gender in any given context are hierarchically organized, that is, some are more powerful and have greater social sanction than others. In the United Kingdom, for example, some forms of masculinity are perhaps much easier to identify with than others because they are socially valued and accepted. Oppressed groups frequently develop their own discourses that work in contra-distinction to dominant ones, but the questions are, can people actively recognize and choose the subject positions they take up, and to what degree are they able to resist the terms of dominant discourses? Much of the debate here turns on the use of the terms 'choice' and 'resistance', and their suitability for analysing processes that are not always conscious or strategic; these issues are discussed in chapters 3, 4 and 5.

What is clear is that individuals are able to bring a considerable amount of self-reflection to bear on the practices and discourses of day-to-day living. In chapter 4 I discuss the ways in which bodily praxis can act as a form of self-reflection that does not always enter the discursive. This clearly raises issues of intentionality and agency, and a number of chapters address the question of agency and its relationship to social determinations. One problem here is how to integrate people's self-images and self-representations with dominant cultural ideologies and/or discourses. Any approach to the analysis of agency must include a consideration of the role of fantasy and desire, both with regard to questions of compliance and resistance and in connection with the construction of a sense of self. These points are elaborated further in chapter 3.

Chapter 5 addresses the politics of identity and its relationship to notions of rights and needs. Rhetorical strategies that draw on categorical and/or stereotypical identities are put into play in circumstances where political and economic resources are at stake. I discuss the redistribution of household resources and how resource flows are determined by a field of power within which identities are constantly being reformulated in categorical terms. The power to define reality is an economic and political power. The experience for individuals of such external definitions has consequences not only for their self-images, but for the material circumstances they find themselves in. I also discuss the way in which notions of agency are predicated upon theories of rights and needs that are implicated in certain identities, and how this varies for persons of different race, gender and class.

Language and the imagination

The construction of a self in relation to other selves involves the enunciation of a series of speaking positions. The taking up of a position on an issue that directly concerns one is always difficult, but it is possible to maintain a critical reflection on one's own experience and on the various positions/locations one chooses to adopt. The position of the anthropologist has always been ambiguous and uneasy because it has depended on a stable division between 'us' and 'them'. This should not obscure the fact, however, that the anthropological 'we' has always been an imaginary category. In chapters 2 and 6, I discuss the fact that at the present time anthropology has at least as much trouble with the unstable nature of the category 'us' as it does with the category 'them'. When cultural theorists and colonial discourse theorists discuss anthropology and its representations of the other, they frequently conflate many complex issues, not least because they appear to assume that all anthropologists are Euro-Americans. This effectively silences what many anthropologists have to say about these problems, and it erases the real difficulties in moving between the poles of a contrastive pair in order to demonstrate where the lines of difference solidify and where they break down. These points are discussed more fully in chapters 1, 2 and 7.

One issue that is raised immediately is the question of where anthropologists get their models from. I suggest in chapters 6 and 7, where I discuss writing and the anthropological imagination, that we do not spend enough time attending to the fantasies and imaginative images of the anthropologists themselves. The anthropological self, like other selves, is one made up through projection and introjection, through identification and recognition and through a desire to belong. How do we construct images of ourselves as anthropologists; and how do the resulting images mark our work and our writing?

This question finds particular force at various times in the book when I address the problem of language and, in particular, the construction of theoretical language. One problem here concerns the degree to which a certain way of conceiving of and talking about gender difference which is prevalent in the social sciences is appropriate for discussing alternative ways of modelling sex/gender difference. This issue is raised in chapters 1 and 2, where I argue that social science and psychoanalytic models are themselves based on local folk models, and the view they produce of sex/gender difference is thus a very ethnocentric one.

Difficulties in this area are compounded because anthropologists and feminists, and indeed different groups of feminists, habitually use a set of terms that they imagine have a common meaning. The terms 'sex', 'gender', 'sexuality', 'gender relations' and 'social relations' are used in a number of quite distinct and very different ways. The result is that, even within the feminist and anthropological communities, we spend a great deal of time talking past each other. Part of the problem can be traced to different intellectual and linguistic traditions, but the rest is probably due to the fact that our use of these terms and the metaphoric resonances they set up for us are grounded in our own bodies and our own experiences. Since we are all gendered individuals, and since we can only speak the social through our selves and through our bodies, it is clear that these terms can never refer to pure concepts.

When writing this book, I constantly came up against the limits of my language and the limits of my imagination. What these texts are about is the struggle to develop a specifically anthropological approach to feminist post-structuralist theory. They are also an attempt to provide a radical critique of anthropology from a feminist perspective. In my writing I change my position and location many times. I have tried, where possible, to reveal the lines of fracture and ambiguity in my own thinking because I have wanted to try to show how much my theorizing is marked through with the specifics of a particular feminist anthropological self.

1

THE DIVISIONS WITHIN: SEX, GENDER AND SEXUAL DIFFERENCE

This essay was originally presented as a paper, and since much of what it discusses turns on problems of position, location, self-representation and representativity, I have decided to leave it, as far as is possible, in its original form. Extensive use of the first-person pronoun is frowned on in the contexts in which I am used to working, but I have deliberately retained it in this text to try to convey a sense of particularity, of myself speaking in a specific context(s). The use of 'we' is a highly politicized act both in anthropology and in feminist contexts. Its use here is intended to convey a sense of audience, that is, of myself speaking to others. But, and much more importantly, it also operates as a mark of interrogation, a fictive unity that reveals the lines of fragmentation at the very moment when it claims affinity.[1]

The original impetus for this paper was a question concerning the way in which feminism had influenced or affected my own work. This perfectly reasonable request engendered in me a feeling of intense panic. My first thought was 'Oh God, how *has* feminism influenced my work?' The root of the anxiety, of course, is one about being found out, being exposed as 'not the real thing', 'not a proper feminist'. The anxiety of failure and lack is not entirely confined to feminists. In fact, it is probably rather a common paranoia among academics. However, what this anxiety raises for me as a feminist is the question of positionality. Feminist politics and feminist practice have always required a clear sense of position and of the politics of location. For one thing, there has been the necessity of speaking out, declaring one's feminist politics within the workplace or the home or the political party or wherever. In addition, the powerful, some- times acrimonious debates within the feminist community itself have demanded that one own up as to where one locates oneself in terms of a variety of carefully drawn and demarcated internal divisions: radical feminist or socialist feminist, for example? These divisions are important because they have guided the political programmes proposed by different groups of feminists, and be- cause they bring already politicized identities into play. They raise, therefore, what I am going to call, after Nancy Miller (1991: 20), the problem of representativity. Who and what do we represent when we speak out, and how do we negotiate the inevitable prob- lem in the social sciences of having to speak about people whilst trying not to speak for them? The question of who speaks for whom and on what basis has given rise in feminist debate to a number of very significant divisions, one of which is the split between theory and practice. The main issue here is how to link theoretical work with political activism. Those who have not seen themselves as theorists have demanded to know what purpose theory serves for them and how readily, if at all, theory takes account of their experi- ences, concerns and struggles. Feminist theory has seemed to many not only arcane, but elitist, racist and/or patriarchal.

Thus, the politics of location make two things abundantly clear. First, that there is no single, homogenous body of feminist theory; and secondly, that the divisions between different groups of women, as well as between practising feminists, make it impossible to assert a commonality based on shared membership in a universal category 'woman'. Such divisions have a particular resonance for me because I work as a social anthropologist. As it happens, I work with and across divisions of race, class, sexuality, ethnicity and religion. I question the purpose of my work, especially my theoreti- cal writing, for the people I work with because I do not find it easy to know of what immediate use it could be to them. I frequently try to deal with this problem, at least in part, by grounding my theoreti- cal thinking in the details of daily life and in the realities of post- colonial political economies. I do not succeed in this as often as I should like, and I tenaciously hold on to what I try to convince myself is an acceptable political position by giving as much space and time to working on issues of agricultural change, women's labour and nutrition as I do to writing on theoretical questions. The gross imbalances of power involved in my research situation mean that at every turn the very fact of writing and talking about other people's lives can never be clearly separated from the question of whether or not one is speaking for them. This is a perennial problem for all feminist social scientists, in spite of a commitment to feminist methodologies and participatory research. Many of my feminist colleagues are very critical of my involvement in anthropology, often projecting on to me their own anxieties about how to deal with issues of race and class, and about how to manage the increasing gap between feminist activism and the academy. I inevitably do the same to them. The most significant impact that feminism has had on my work has been to create a space in which I must continually engage with these issues of positionality and representativity. I want to take up a very small part of this theme in this essay and discuss the way in which theoretical treatments of sex, gender and sexual difference are connected to what it is that unites and what it is that divides us as women and as feminists.

The assertion of the non-universal status of the category 'woman' is by now almost a commonplace. Anthropology has had a particular historical role in the development of feminist theory because of its contribution to the critical reworking of the category 'woman'. In the 1970s feminists outside anthropology drew readily on the cross-cultural data provided by anthropological research to establish variability in gender and gender roles, and thus provide substantive content for the feminist position that gender was socially constructed and not biologically determined. However, cross-cultural variability in the social construction of gender could not and did not account for women's universal subordination, and in order to remedy this, anthropology developed two very important comparative theories.

The first asserted that women everywhere were associated with nature, partly as a result of their reproductive functions, while men were associated with culture. It was suggested that the devaluing of nature in relation to culture accounted for the hierarchical relations between women and men (see Ortner, 1974). The second theory emphasized that women were inferior to men because they were linked to the domestic sphere, once again in consequence of their role in reproduction and child care, whilst men were associated with the public sphere of social life (see Rosaldo, 1974). These comparative theories of women's subordination were not long-lived. The categories of nature, culture, public and private were themselves found to be historically and culturally variable, and the homologies posited between these categories and the categories of gender difference were revealed to be far from universal (see Moore, 1988: 13–30; MacCormack and Strathern, 1980; Strathern, 1984; and Rosaldo, 1980). What is important about these two comparative theories of women's subordination is that they attempted to provide socially, as opposed to biologically, based accounts of women's position in society and of the origins of gender difference. The preconditions for this project were, of course, that the biological and the social had already been separated from each other as explanations for the origins of gender difference. Whatever role biology was playing, it was not determining gender.

The very fact that these comparative theories were social rather than biological in their determinations opened them to critical reinterpretation by feminists of colour, feminists from the developing world and lesbian feminists. They challenged the notion of the universal category 'woman' and the assumption of underlying commonalities of existence for all women. Trans-cultural and trans-historical patterns of female subordination were rejected, and theoretical concepts were reformulated.[2] In the social sciences, at least, this produced a crisis both about the political purpose and organization of a feminist politics which did not appear to have a coherent constituency and about the status of analytical models of gender. In general, it would probably be fair to say that many responded to the latter crisis by asserting the necessity for culturally and historically specific analyses. We could look for commonalities between well-specified situations, but we would never be able to state in advance what the consequences of the intersections of race, class and gender, for example, would be. What is interesting about this crisis is that it generated a simultaneous move towards pluralism and specificity. An enormous range of empirical outcomes and theoretical positions were produced as a result of having to reduce the scope of any model or analytical statement to a particular situation. We now recognize this development as part of a general critique of universalizing theories, metanarratives and totalizing typologies. The current debate is, of course, one about whether we locate the origins of this movement in post-structuralism and deconstructionism or in feminism.

However, as regards feminist theory in the social sciences, the shift in methods of gender analysis towards a specificity which would account for a plurality of experiences and contexts was not as radical as it seemed. One fixed position remained and that was the division between sex and gender. Gender was seen as socially constructed, but underlying that idea was a notion that although gender was not determined by biology, it *was* the social elaboration in specific contexts of the obvious facts of biological sex difference. It did not matter that almost everyone recognized that both biology and culture were historically and culturally variable concepts, as were the relations between them. The problem was that the elaboration of the social determinations and entailments of gender in all their specificity had effectively left the relationship between sex and gender very under-theorized.

Recent work in anthropology has returned to this question of the relationship between sex and gender. Sylvia Yanagisako and Jane Collier (1987) have suggested that the radical separation of sex and gender characteristic of feminist anthropology is a specific and rather pervasive ethnocentrism. They argue that it is part of a western folk model which dominates anthropological theorizing and, like so many of the other binary categorizations in anthropology – nature/culture, public/private – it does not stand up to cross-cultural examination. In many ways this simply marks the impact of neo-Foucauldian thinking in anthropology. It is worth recalling here Foucault's argument in *The History of Sexuality* (vol. i) that 'sex' is an effect rather than an origin and that, far from being a given and essential unity, it is, as a category, the product of specific discursive practices:

> the notion of 'sex' made it possible to group together, in an artificial unity, anatomical elements, biological functions, conducts, sensations, and pleasures, and it enabled one to make use of this fictitious unity as a causal principle, an omnipresent meaning; sex was thus able to function as a unique signifier and as a universal signified. (1978: 154)

Foucault's basic argument is that the notion of 'sex' does not exist prior to its determination within a discourse in which its constellations of meanings are specified, and that therefore bodies have no 'sex' outside discourses in which they are designated as sexed. Consequently, the construction of fixed binary sexes, with fixed categorical differences, is the effect of a specific discourse. What is more, if binary sex is an effect of discourse, then it cannot be considered as a unitary essentialism and, more importantly, it cannot be recognized as invariant or natural. This is, in essence, the argument Thomas Laqueur makes so elegantly in his recent book (1990) and two quite radical positions follow from this point.

First, in terms of anthropological discourse the distinction between sex and gender on which feminist anthropology has rested its case falls away. As Judith Butler (1990) points out in her reading of the above passage from Foucault, perhaps there is no distinction to be made between sex and gender after all. The second point, which follows from the first, is that, as Yanagisako and Collier (1987) assert, we cannot necessarily assume that binary biological sex everywhere provides the universal basis for the cultural categories 'male' and 'female'. If gender constructs are culturally variable, then so are the categories of sexual difference. This is not the first time in anthropology or anywhere else that the fixed binary categories of sex have been interrogated; one only needs to point to the research that exists on 'the third sex', hermaphrodism and androgeny.[3] But recent work in anthropology has a rather different purpose.

We know that the recognition of anatomical differences between women and men does not necessarily produce a discrete, fixed, binary categorization of sex in the manner of western discourse. Ethnographic material suggests that the differences between women and men which people in other cultures naturalize and locate in the human body and in features of the physical and cosmological environment are not necessarily those which correspond to the constellation of features on which western discourse bases its categorizations. For example, the social differences between women and men may be located in the body as natural differences, as in situations described by anthropologists working in Nepal, where the differences between the female and the male are conceived of as the difference between flesh and bone.[4] However, these differences of gender are said to be located in all bodies, thus collapsing the distinction between sexed bodies and socially constructed genders usually maintained in anthropological discourse. The female and the male, as flesh and bone, are necessary features of bodily identity. This produces a discursive space where theories of social (gender) difference are grounded in the physiology of the body, and thus function as part of the biological facts of sex difference.

This is, of course, very close to Foucault's own project, which is concerned with how it is that sexual differences and the category of sex are constructed within discourse as necessary features of bodily identity. In western discourse, it appears, it is not just that we need to have a body in order to have a sex, but that we need a sex so as to have a body. This rather strange way of thinking, of modelling the relationship between bodies and the categories of sexual difference, is precisely that which is most readily undermined by ethnographic material. Many of the differences which concern people around the world are internal to bodies, that is, within them rather than between them. The question is, are we to speak of these differences as differences of sex or of gender? This point is difficult to grasp for many of us because we have the gravest difficulty in understanding categories of sex and notions of sexual difference which do not correspond neatly to discrete physical bodies already designated as sexually differentiated. Sex, then, as far as we understand it within the terms of western discourse, is something which differentiates between bodies, while gender is the set of variable social constructions placed upon those differentiated bodies. It is precisely this formula which obscures rather than illuminates when it comes to the cross-cultural analysis of sex, sexual difference and gender. In many instances, as I have already suggested, gender differences are internal to all bodies and are part of the process through which bodies are sexed. In such situations it is far from apparent how we should distinguish sex from gender, and, even more problematic, it is unclear exactly what gender as a concept or a category refers to. This argument is quite different from those which have been made about the 'third sex', hermaphrodism and androgeny.

The instability – potential instability – of the category 'gender' in cross-cultural analysis is an alarming prospect. When we talk in general terms about discourses on gender and on the relationship between sex and gender, even if by this we only really mean to say different ideas about sex and gender, we still have to ask ourselves, whose discourses are we referring to? At one time anthropology subscribed to the view that each culture had its own model of gender, its own definitions of the categories female and male. This view, which was much reinforced by a predominantly

Durkheimian view of culture and by the kind of liberal cultural relativism still prevalent in the discipline, has changed in recent years as anthropologists have moved towards working with models of culture which stress conflict and indeterminacy, and as they concentrate more on the differences within cultures as opposed to simply between them.[5] However, it does not solve the problem of how to link what we might call dominant cultural models of gender to the specific experiences and situations of particular groups or individuals within that social context. This is not, of course, a problem which is confined to anthropology, but it raises once again the problems of positionality and representativity.

One set of difficulties here is about how the experiences of race, sexuality and class, as well as other forms of salient difference, transform the experience of gender. But there are additional problems about how we are to conceptualize and analyse the overdetermined relationships between dominant and sub-dominant discourses on gender, the body, sexuality and sexual difference. These questions become particularly acute when we acknowledge that they are crucial not only in and for our work, but in and for our lives. What relationship do feminist understandings of gender have to dominant gender models and ideologies; can the former ever be entirely free of the latter; is this what we are striving for? This is a matter of subjectivity and self-identity, as well as a matter of politics. When we are busy discussing other people's discourses on gender, their views about the body, their gender identities and subjectivities, how easy do we find it to produce the kind of analysis which we would like to see applied to ourselves?

As Adrienne Rich remarked:

> Perhaps we need a moratorium on saying 'the body'. For it's also possible to abstract 'the body'. When I write 'the body', I see nothing in particular. To write 'my body' plunges me into lived experience, particularity ... To say 'the body' lifts me away from what has given me primary perspective. To say 'my body' reduces the temptation to grandiose assertions. (1986: 215)

By 'grandiose assertions' Rich means presumably universalizing, comparative theories. As a lesbian feminist, Rich is only too well aware that the dominant discourses on gender, the body and sexuality prevalent in her own cultural setting do not fit her personal understanding of these categories and/or processes very closely. Lesbians, like many other groups, have evolved their own dis- courses, what some have termed sub-dominant or alternative dis- courses, on these issues. It is on this basis that writers talk of different kinds of experience – 'the lesbian experience' or 'the black experience', for example – and seek in terms of feminist theory to establish the grounds for theoretical approaches based on positionality and representativity. However, the problem is not just how to recognize the existence of specific groups who may have alternative perspectives and may not subscribe to dominant dis- courses within any particular setting. The more pressing problem with regard to gender, the body and sexual difference is to work out what bearing social and cultural discourses have on individual experience.

This is, of course, simply a modern version of an old problem in sociology and anthropology about the relationship between the individual and society. In anthropology this problem has often been run in terms of the relationship between dominant cultural symbols and the individual's understanding and interpretation of them. This is a key issue in feminist theory, where feminist standpoint theory invites us to take women's experiences as a starting point for analy- sis (see, for example, Harding, 1987, and chapter 4 of this volume). Standpoint theory assumes that women have a different perspective from men, and that different groups of women will also differ in their standpoints. In this sense it privileges groups over individuals, but a more radical reading of its premises would suggest that we all of us have different experiences and understandings of cultural discourses, symbols and institutions. The question is how much any of us share with each other.

The specific and the universal, the particular and the comparative – how are these two polarities to be brought into conjunction with each other? I have always been a supporter of the specific and the particular over the universal and the comparative, and I have always assumed that this is the result of my experience of research in Africa. However, I was listening to Catherine MacKinnon lectur- ing recently on women and human rights.[6] MacKinnon holds to a radical feminist version of standpoint theory; in her work she con- stantly emphasizes what it is that women, in the global sense, share, and her work has been extensively criticized on precisely this point. She was talking about the mass rape and enforced impregnation of women in Croatia and Bosnia-Herzegovina. She argued simply that these crimes have been and continue to be practised on women in many different times and places, and without erasing or ignoring the specifics of what is going on in the former Yugoslavia, it is important to recognize that women suffer these crimes at the hands of men and they do so because they are women. Women are in fact *universal* in their *particularity*. It was very hard at that moment to deny the force of her argument, or even to think of any compelling reason why I should ever have disagreed with it. Women do fear sexual violence. If we want some empirical justification for such a universalizing assertion, it is only a matter of looking at the various women's grassroots organizations around the world and at what they are campaigning against.

Rosi Braidotti, starting from very different assumptions, makes an argument which has strong parallels with MacKinnon's. She speaks of a vision of women as a *collective singularity*, where this notion is intended to provide a provisional platform for the support of 'women's real and multiple struggles' (1991: 132). But when we examine her argument and consider what she founds her collective singularity on, we find the connections with MacKinnon's argument quite evident. For example, at one point she says: 'It is on the basis of their shared experience as bio-culturally female beings that women have started to speak in their own voice, distancing it from masculine experience' (1991: 139). Bodies. It all has something to do with bodies.

Is it really the case that our similarities are grounded in our bodies? This is an example of a moment when the personal comes into lived relation with the theoretical. I find that my antipathy even to simply posing this question is so great that I have to remind myself not to grind my teeth. And yet, I know that the recent return to the body in feminist theory and the efforts on the part of many researchers to reclaim the female body and the feminine – partly as a protest against the disembodied nature of the social constructionist discourse on the body – seems to many to offer real hope and potential. This return to the body is not a straightforward one, because some researchers want to distinguish between different types of female body. Some do not want to reduce the female body to its sexual and reproductive functions and they want to be able to mark a female body which is not the maternal body. For others, the primary connection is between mothers and daughters, or mothers and children, and they would like to be able to celebrate the maternal in the female body.[7]

French feminists associated with the school of *l'écriture feminine* have been accused of biological essentialism, though their work has recently been re-evaluated on this point (Brennan, 1989; Schor, 1989). Rosi Braidotti, in particular, argues that this charge of essentialism is false and that the feminine libidinal economy discussed in this work has taken on board the fundamental episte-mological insight of post-structuralism and psychoanalysis which is that the body is a 'cultural artefact' (1991: 219, 243). Braidotti suggests that what is hopeful about a return to the female body is that it signals a recognition of the embodied nature of sub-jectivity. However, there is a distinction to be made here between her argument and a straightforward neo-Foucauldian or social constructionist one, because she eschews any attempt to sever the body from the biological and claim that it is just a social construction or a social field, nothing other than an effect of discourse (1991: 131, 243). This point is worth making because it is the case that a radical social constructionist position, such as that espoused by Judith Butler (1990) in her recent book, does risk positing the body as a blank surface on which the social becomes inscribed, thus suggesting in some sense that the body is pre-social.[8]

Braidotti argues that what is truly revolutionary about a return to the female body is the notion of speaking from the body, with all that this implies both about the specificity of positionality and the embodied, material nature of one's relation with the world. Much of her inspiration seems to come from a reading of Adrienne Rich against the writings of the *écriture feminine* school, and it is from the former that she derives her term 'feminine corpor(e)ality'. Rich writes in *Of Woman Born* (1976: 39–40):

> In order to live a fully human life we require not only control of our bodies . . . ; we must touch the unity and resonance of our physicality, our bond with the natural order, the corporeal ground of our intelligence.

Rich takes the woman-to-woman bond as the grounds for subjec-tivity and for social relations. Braidotti tries to take the argument about feminine corpor(e)ality a stage further, and she stresses a notion of the body as an interface, a threshold between the material and the symbolic. The body is, therefore, not an essence nor indeed a form of anatomical destiny, but rather it is 'one's primary location in the world, one's primary situation in reality' (Braidotti, 1991: 219).

Thus, speaking from the body would be a way of acknowledging women's position in the world, their difference from men, their particularity. It would also be a way of stressing simultaneously women's material and symbolic relation to their world. Such a view of the body could in principle, though Braidotti does not elaborate on this point, deal both with the politics of reproduction and sexual violence and with the symbolic construction of sexual difference, including the discursive overdetermination of the category 'woman'. Braidotti is sensitive to the charges of exclusion and un-warranted universalism that could be levelled at this theory, but by stressing the materiality and specificity of the body as a location for subjectivity she hopes to take account of the differences between women, whilst allowing for what MacKinnon would term their *universal particularity*.

There are some interesting parallels here with more recent work in biology. The radical separation of biology and culture is some-thing many biologists would no longer hold to. A more contempor-ary view of human biology would stress that biology enables culture, while culture brings about biological change. In what now sound like rather old-fashioned terms we could say that biology and culture are in a dialectical relationship. In this version of biology the body is indeed an interface, a threshold, a mediator. Perhaps we are arriving at a situation where the metaphors of the biological and the social sciences are going to come into some kind of conjunction or relation with each other.

Overall, we might argue that the view of the body espoused by Rosi Braidotti has considerable potential. In particular, its welding of French and North American feminist theory allows it to occupy a rather creative discursive space. But this notion of the body does still provide difficulties and these arise predominantly, I suggest, because of the influence of psychoanalytic thought on the scholars on whom Braidotti draws. The crux of the issue is what is the ontological status of the body, and beyond that what is the ontologi-cal status of sexual difference? In order to proceed much further with this discussion, we have to recognize the degree to which we as feminists have a tendency to talk past each other once we begin to speak of sex, gender and sexual difference. One starting point is to note that sexual difference for French feminist scholars is not sex and it is not gender.[9] It is, I think, a rather intermediate term. This is because much of their work draws on psychoanalytic thought and starts with the premise that one must acquire a sexed identity. But however one might theorize the stages involved in that acquisition, it is not the same thing as anatomical sex, nor is it the same thing as acquiring a gender.

Braidotti's return to the female body reinscribes binary sexual difference, and makes the inevitability of a mutually exclusive categorization the basis for women's engagement with the world. In this sense it does not matter that she can deal with the charge of universalism by providing the space for an embodied subjectivity that can be historically and culturally specific, because what she cannot do is to abandon the originary nature of the sexual difference which grounds her theory of the body. The question is, does this matter? Perhaps there is a case for asserting the primacy of sexual difference if we want to describe women in their *particularity*, and especially if we want to treat issues of domination and power.

However, as many others have pointed out, there are very serious difficulties with asserting a primary, ontological status for sexual difference: principally, the exclusion of other forms of difference, notably race and class; and the reinscription of the binary categorization of sexual difference which makes the feminine the male 'other' and institutes a relation of hierarchy. Theories which posit the primacy of sexual difference are in fact vulnerable to criticism because in order for the assertion of primacy to be convincing, they have to be abstract and decontextualized. At the first moment that the question 'Whose sexed identity?' is asked, it becomes apparent that the reality of such a lived identity is that it cannot be experienced in a pure form.

When has gender ever been pure, untainted by other forms of difference, other relations of inequality? Lives are shaped by a multiplicity of differences, differences which may be perceived categorically but are lived relationally. The concepts of sexual difference and gender difference collide at this moment and cannot usefully be separated again, though they never become and cannot become identical. And as for gender discourse, there is no discourse on gender outside the discourses of race and class and ethnicity and sexuality and so on. The point, then, is that although, in theory, we could all live the categorizations of our bodies and our identities in different ways – as Braidotti implies – we would still have to acknowledge that, in terms of the theory as posited, our bodies would be primarily differentiated in relation to a binary sexual economy which would be prior to all other forms of difference.

Perhaps the problem is not really one about bodies at all, but about identities, or rather about how we conceive of the relationship between the two. This is a problem which has been formulated for at least some of us in a very specific way by psychoanalysis. Psycho-analytic theory is, as has been remarked, an historically and cul-turally specific theory, just like any other. But the processes of identity acquisition which it proposes are intended to have univer-sal application, and the relationships between anatomy, sexuality and identity which it validates are presented as marking the path of non-pathological development. The rigidity of the sexed categories that psychoanalysis provides is open to question. Jacqueline Rose for one has argued that psychoanalytic theory does not work with a notion of fixed and immutable identities, and that it has been one of the few places in western culture where it has been possible to realize that women 'do not slip painlessly into their roles as women, if indeed they do at all' (1983: 9). However, in spite of these more liberal interpretations, which argue that psychoanalysis takes sexual difference as something to be explained rather than assumed, it is still the case that psychoanalytic theory insists that in order to become a member of a social order we must make an identification with either the category 'woman' or the category 'man'. This is the nub of the matter. What does psychoanalytic theory intend when it says that we must identify with one or other of these categories? Is it really proposed that we should take these categories to be discur-sively produced and therefore variable across space and time? There is much talk about how it should be possible to imagine a signifying economy which does not take the phallus as the primary signifier, but this is seen as a potentiality rather than an actuality. From the point of view of cross-cultural analysis, it can be argued that Lacan's law of the father is ethnocentric and that, since it is an abstract and decontextualized theory of signification and takes no account of any form of difference except that of sex, it is exclusionary in a number of ways.

Lacan has always been credited with cleansing Freud of biologisms, and some of his own ideas about the body and its relation to subjectivity are suggestive. Lacan moves away from

Freud's idea of sexual drives as given in biological development to an analysis of such drives through the functioning of language and linguistic processes. For Lacan, drives are not biologically determined, but rather are constituted in processes of signification. Lacan treats the body in an analogous fashion, suggesting that the body as it is experienced and perceived by the child is fragmentary, a body-in-bits-and-pieces. Out of this biological chaos of sensation and physiological activity will be constructed a lived anatomy, a psychic map of the body which is given not by biology, but by significations and fantasies (both personal and collective) of the body (Grosz, 1990: 43–4). Elizabeth Grosz describes 'this body' in the following way:

> Bound up within parental fantasies long before the child is ever born, the child's body is divided along lines of special meaning or significance, independent of biology. The body is lived in accordance with an individual's and a culture's *concepts* of biology. (1990: 44)

This sounds a little like Foucault with the psychic and the cultural added. Lacan's lived anatomy is an imaginary one, a unity created out of the internalizations of self – other relations. The 'body-image' is an effect of the highly particular meanings that the body has been endowed with by individuals, by cultures and – according to Lacan – by the nuclear family. One cannot accept this proposition about the nuclear family uncritically, but what seems to be implied here is that the body-image or corporeal schema is the result of the internalization of the body-image of others, particularly the primary carer. Overall, what is significant about this body-image is that it is neither natural nor cultural, neither individual nor social; rather it is a threshold term occupying both positions (Grosz, 1990: 46).

There are some resonances here with Braidotti's 'feminine corpor(e)ality', though in order to provide a workable theory of embodied subjectivity we would need to combine Braidotti's emphasis on materiality with Lacan's insistence on the symbolic. This might prove extremely difficult, not to say risky, since there is nothing that links Braidotti's female body to Lacan's feminine, except some residual and unresolved problem about anatomy. The problem is that the female and the feminine are not the same thing. At this point the concepts of sex, gender and sexual difference all collide together. The meanings of these terms begin to escape us, and they do so largely because they are decontextualized. It is only in the context of racial discrimination, religious intolerance, neo-imperial politics and other concrete socio-economic determinations that we know what distinguishes sex from gender, that we understand the economy of sexual difference, that we come to grips with the material referents of the symbolic. The potential for developing a feminist theory of embodied subjectivity which could and would take account of race, class, sexuality and other forms of difference certainly exists. However, it is likely to remain permanently out of reach whilst we insist that sex, gender and sexual difference are foundational in some sense, either as categories or as sets of relations. In so far as the theories of the body I have been discussing rest on post-structuralist assumptions they are clearly anti-foundationalist; though my point is that they are not really so because they work on the assumption that bodies are already divided into two mutually exclusive categories. Binary biological sex provides the basis for the cultural categories 'male' and 'female'. The shifting and unstable nature of the sexed identity proposed by Lacan is always mapped on to and mapped out in terms of a pre-existing categorization of sex. This may not matter, of course, if what we really want to do is to work out some kind of critical practice, that is, a space for critical reflection on and political action around these issues, rather than a new metatheory.

As an anthropologist, it is the pre-existing categorization of sex – that somehow, in the hands of theorists, transmutes itself first into sexual difference and thence into gender – which is the stumbling block. Much new work on the gendering of body parts, bodily substances and social acts makes it clear that there is no one-to-one correspondence between sex, gender and sexual difference understood in the terms of western discourse. As I suggested earlier, individual persons, whilst having recognizable biological features, might not have discrete and singular genders in the sense that feminist discourse has conventionally understood that term. Anna Meigs has argued, on the basis of her research with the Hua people of the Eastern Highlands of Papua New Guinea, that individuals are classified by external anatomical features, but that they are also classified according to the amount of certain male and female substances they have in their bodies. These substances are thought to be transferable between the genital classes through eating, heterosexual sex and everyday casual contact (Meigs, 1990: 108–9). The binary categories 'female' and 'male' are thus not discrete ones and nor are they premised on the discrete binary categorization of biological sex differences evidenced by external genitalia.

The Hua insist that the gender of a person changes over their lifetime as their body takes on more of the substances and fluids transferred by the other sex. On the basis of what Meigs says, the Hua would appear to have a pre-existing categorization of sex, since they classify substances as sexed according to the kinds of bodies they originate in. Semen, for example, is a male substance. However, the question is, how well are their theories of sex, gender and sexual difference represented by theoretical models premised on European and North American folk models? Perhaps it does not matter that in order to make alternative gender models intelligible to our students, colleagues and readers we have to rework them in terms which thoroughly misrepresent them. Thereby, I may add, making them appear even more exotic. But there is an additional point, because one of the things revealed by alternative models for thinking and living the connections of sex, gender and sexual difference is that European and North American models are probably not well served by the prevailing theories either. Many people find that their theories of sexual difference and their experience of gendered identities do not correspond well to discrete binary categories. There has been some recognition of this in recent theoretical work on gender, where writers have begun to emphasize the performative aspects of gender identity and the possibilities that exist for the subversion of categorical identities (see, for example, Butler, 1990, and Garber, 1992).

This emphasis on performance is welcome, but it does not seem very revolutionary from an anthropological point of view. This is because ethnographic material suggests that gender categorizations are often based on roles – that is, on what women and men do – rather than on anatomy. The North American Berdache is now a rather well-known example of a third gender categorization which counters the one-to-one equivalence of the binary categories of sex and gender; and a man usually becomes a Berdache by assuming the tasks and roles of a woman (W. Williams, 1986; H. Whitehead, 1981; Roscoe, 1988). There is considerable emphasis in the anthropological literature on gender as performed and its relation to the symbolic construction of gender. More recent work stresses that these different aspects of gender are perhaps best seen as mutually co-existent, but sometimes conflicting models of, or discourses on, gender. Where discourses exist that focus on the absolute and irreducible nature of sexual difference, there is no particular reason to privilege them over other discourses or to accord them some kind of foundational status. What is essential is to examine those contexts in which certain discourses become appropriate and powerful. Marriage ceremonies, for example, are sometimes situations in which sexual difference is stressed; whereas philosophical discussion may produce a very different account, underplaying the role of women and men in biological reproduction and emphasizing their essential similarities, especially through the course of biographical time. Ethnographic accounts often give a very vivid sense of people's perceptions of their 'lived anatomies' and of how understandings of bodies, gender identities and sexual difference are given substance through involvement in repetitive daily tasks and through the concrete nature of social relationships. From this perspective it is hardly surprising that age, class, race, sexuality and religion completely alter the experience of a 'lived anatomy', of what it is that sex, gender and sexual difference signify. What performance is all about, of course, is gender relations.

'Gender relations' is not, however, a term widely used by theorists who derive their inspiration from post-structuralism or from the writings of Lacan. Conversely, we should note that anthropologists rarely use the term 'sexual difference' unless they mean biological sex, and they never use the phrase 'sexual relations' unless they mean sexual intercourse. We can see once again how easy it is for us all to talk past one another. This is particularly the case when we think about performance and gender relations, and the connection of both to a notion of embodied subjectivity.

Lacan explicitly states that the subject divided in language is a subject constituted in language; but by language he does not mean social discourse, he means instead a system of signification, a system of signs. More problematic still is the fact that the Lacanian subject should not be confused either with the person or with the self. The assumption of a sexed subject position is a prerequisite for agency and for self-identity, and as such subjectivity is an attribute of the self, but subjects are not individuals. It is for this reason that Lacanian ideas about the constitution of subjectivity – in spite of the liberating release they provide from Cartesian views of the subject and its role in the production of knowledges – are likely to give us

very little insight into the experience of being a gendered individual. To do that, we would need to link Lacanian ideas about the
constitution of subjectivity to social discourses and discursive practices. This is precisely what a number of feminists have tried to do,
most notably perhaps Teresa de Lauretis (1986). The issue here, of
course, is that the sexed subject and the gendered individual are not
one and the same. There is a gap and it is this gap which the notions
of embodied subjectivity and copor(e)al femininity are designed
to fill.

De Lauretis tries to bridge the same gap by stressing notions of
intersubjectivity and relationality. She makes use of the insights of
Lacanian theory, but her concern is with an 'I' understood as a
complicated field of competing subjectivities and competing identities. This 'I' is most certainly a concrete individual and one who is
engaged in relations with others (1986). Such a view of subjectivity
does not privilege gender over all other forms of difference, but
because of its stress on intersubjectivity and on social relations it is
perfectly compatible with a notion of embodied subjectivity, as well
as with ideas about performance. De Lauretis argues convincingly
that differences between women may be better understood as differences within women. In other words, that the differences of race,
class, sexuality and so on are constitutive of gender identity. As De
Lauretis says:

> the female subject is a site of differences; differences that are not only
> sexual or only racial, economic, or (sub)cultural, but all of these
> together and often enough at odds with one another . . . once it is
> understood . . . that these differences not only constitute each
> woman's consciousness and subjective limits but all together define
> the female subject of feminism in its very specificity . . . these
> differences . . . cannot be again collapsed into a fixed identity, a same-
> ness of all women as Woman, or a representation of Feminism as a
> coherent and available image. (1986: 14–15)

Difference is, of course, a relational concept, and it is always
experienced relationally in terms of political discrimination, inequalities of power and forms of domination. There is, therefore,
nothing useful to be said about gender outside the concrete
specificity of gender relations. This very specificity guarantees that
gender itself does not exist outside its material and symbolic inter-

sections with other forms of difference. In fact, I would suggest for the time being that we might be better off working back towards sex, gender, sexual difference and the body, rather than taking them as a set of starting points. If our *universal particularity* is to be significant, and if we are to achieve anything as a *collective singularity*, then we might best strive towards an understanding of embodied subjectivity which does not privilege gender and sexual difference unduly just because we are so uncertain about what else it is, if anything, that we share.

2

EMBODIED SELVES: DIALOGUES BETWEEN ANTHROPOLOGY AND PSYCHOANALYSIS

Issues of human identity, intention and agency have always engaged the attention of philosophers. In recent years they have become the focus of anthropological enquiry. One result of this has been an explosion of interest in local and/or indigenous concepts of person and self. What is interesting about this research is that although it has developed contemporaneously with the anthropology of gender, there has been little attempt to bring these two fields of enquiry together. Indigenous concepts of the person and the self are presented, most often, as gender neutral, but on closer examination it is clear that the implicit model for the person in much ethnographic writing is, in fact, an adult male.[1] The apparent resistance to joining these two domains of enquiry is curious for a number of reasons. First, anthropologists have long recognized that there are many instances in which women and men are thought to be different sorts of persons because their capacity for agency depends on their gender identity. Secondly, in much anthropological writing on the person an explicit concern with the boundaries and physical constitution of the person, and with the associated questions of agency and intention, raises immediate questions about the relationship between personal identity and embodiment. One such link is evident, for example, in the case of procreation beliefs, were ideas about the physical make-up of the body are closely connected both to ideas about the nature of the person and to ideas about gender (see chapter 1). Thirdly, the demarcation of the anthropology of the person/self from the anthropology of gender seems particularly curious given that psychoanalysis provides western culture with a model of the acquisition of human subjectivity and identity which is crucially dependent on sexual difference.[2] The subject of psychoanalysis is always a sexed subject.

Anthropology and its theories of person and self

Anthropologists have never assumed that the western concepts of the person and the self are universal, and, almost uniquely among academic disciplines, they have the data to show that this is the case.[3] However, in the face of recent post-structuralist and deconstructionist critiques of the unified, rational subject of western humanist discourse, anthropologists have remained perversely silent; they have scarcely contributed to the debate at all.[4]

This silence is hard to interpret. There are those who would point to the hostility displayed towards post-structuralist and deconstructionist approaches in the discipline. The strange fact of the matter is that while most anthropologists are strongly socially constructionist and, less often, culturally relativist in their thinking, they have a firm allegiance to the empirical nature of ethnographic facts. The result is a fruitful, but uneasy tension between social constructionism and empiricism.

The ambivalent relations between empiricism and social constructionism apparent in anthropological writing and theorizing are partly the product of the political liberalism which historically has informed much anthropological thinking. This is not to say that all anthropologists are liberals – such a statement would patently be false – but rather that anthropology has maintained a commitment to the sovereign nature of individuals, to the coherence and rationality of their beliefs, values and life-ways and to their right for self-determination. In this context it is quite unsurprising that anthropology – or rather a significant number of its practitioners – should be resistant to post-structuralist and deconstructionist attempts to undermine the Cartesian cogito, the 'I' who authors experience of self and of the world, the essence at the core of identity. This resistance should be understood from at least two perspectives. First, there is the understandable reluctance, equally evident in the writings of many feminist theorists (for example, Tress, 1988; Flax, 1987), to relinquish the idea that persons in other cultures are rational, unified individuals, in favour of a view of the subject and of subjectivity which stresses its shifting, imaginary and conflicting nature. This latter view, while absolutely harmless for the average white male academic, could so easily become a pathological characterization of others. Secondly, there is the question of the anthropologists themselves and of their role in the production of anthropological knowledge. Anthropologists have historically based their knowledge of another culture on their experience of that culture: an experience which is both authentic and unique (see chapter 6). Post-structuralist and deconstructionist readings of the subject emphasize that the 'I' does not author experience, that there is no singular essence at the core of each individual which makes them what they are and which guarantees the authenticity of their knowledge of self and of the world. It is clear that from both these perspectives post-structuralist and deconstructionist accounts of the subject appear to threaten the anthropological project.

Appropriately enough, however, this threat is more apparent than real. One way in which this can be made evident is through an examination of anthropological findings and arguments about the person and the self cross-culturally. Anthropological work on the self, known variously as indigenous psychology, ethnopsychology and cultural psychology, embodies many different approaches and philosophical positions. Such differences frequently oscillate around questions of universality. A large body of work draws on the writings of Irving Hallowell (1971) and G. H. Mead (1934). In such work the capacity for self-awareness, the ability to distinguish self from other (self-identity) and the apprehension of self-continuity are thought to be essential for basic human and cultural functioning. In short, they are considered as universal attributes of the self. These universal attributes, however, do not imply anything about the local views of the self which will be prevalent in any particular culture. Many anthropologists have been very specific about the fact that these universal attributes underpin all local conceptions, but are not to be confused with a western concept of the self. The western concept of the self is simply another local model.

Anthropologists remain very divided over the degree to which local, culturally constructed models of the self can be seen to be constitutive of psychological processes *per se*. The controversy rumbles on: some argue that processes such as memory do not make much sense outside the culturally constructed concepts of memory and the way in which those concepts determine the experience of memory, while others insist that memory is a function that operates and/or exists independently of the way in which it might be conceptualized in specific contexts.

Less controversial is the anthropological recognition that indigenous or local concepts of the self vary in the way in which they conceptualize the relationship between self and non-self, the degree to which mind (if it exists at all) is separated from body and the manner in which agency and motivation are conceptualized as arising internally or externally to the self. More importantly, perhaps, concepts like the unconscious are seen, by some, to be highly culturally specific, as are ideas about the bounded and unitary nature of the self. These kinds of arguments in anthropology are not only supported by cross-cultural analysis, but have gained credibility through their comparison with historical data on the changing nature of western concepts of the self over time. Anthropology's slow recognition of variability in western discourses, on this and other matters, has been due, by and large, to the discipline's need for a stable set of concepts, categories and discourses through which to view other people's cultures. However, the acknowledgement of variability does not entirely dispose of the unease which many anthropologists feel regarding social constructionist arguments. In other words, just because people do not speak of having an unconscious and do not discursively or practically recognize the existence and functioning of the unconsciousness, this does not mean that they do not have an unconscious or that unconscious processes do not influence their developmental psychology.

Nominalism may be a perennial problem in anthropology, but it is equally implausible to suggest that discourses and discursive practices are not constitutive of experience. It seems clear that since all psychic and developmental processes are relational, then the nature of the relationship between self and other(s), and the matrix of social relations and symbolic systems within which that relationship is conducted, must play a key role in the development of the self and of subjectivity. It appears pertinent, therefore, that in many contexts people do not believe that selves and persons are bounded and they do not believe that embodiment is the essence of identity.

Germaine Dieterlen argued in the 1940s that the Dogon believe that a person remains in a permanent relation with other persons, and with aspects of the natural world, in such a way that these human and non-human elements are constitutive of the person (1941). Similar arguments, drawing on Mauss, have been made, of course, for a number of African societies (for example, Lienhardt, 1985). Also in the 1940s, Maurice Leenhardt argued that the Canaque of New Caledonia regard the person as being connected to other persons, both human and non-human, material and non-material. What is more, the body is conceived of as a temporary locus, and not as a source of individual identity (Leenhardt, [1947] 1979). Similarly, Anne Strauss's work on the Cheyenne emphasizes that the Cheyenne self participates in, and cannot be defined by contrast with, other Cheyenne selves. Furthermore, the concept of person extends beyond human beings to include other non-human persons. For the Cheyenne, relationships with non-human persons are crucial for the development of the self. The categorical identification between persons and human beings on which western social science and many other indigenous western discourses are based is ruptured (Strauss, 1982: 124–5). In addition, the assumed relationship between self, self-identity and experience has been brought into question by a number of writers. Jean Smith has suggested that for the Maori it was generally not the self which encompassed experience, but experience which encompassed the self. According to Smith, the Maori individual was made up of various independent organs of experience, and these organs each reacted to external stimuli independently of the self. Thus, the self was not viewed as controlling experience, and an individual's experience was not felt to be integral to the self (J. Smith, 1981: 152).

This brief review of some local theories of the person and the self raises two very interesting points. The first concerns the extent to which persons who are not thought to be separate from other persons (both human and non-human) can be conceived of as individuals. In an earlier period in anthropology it was fashionable to follow Mauss in arguing that the self was a social product, and that in primitive societies it was relatively undifferentiated. The individual was seen as a modern construct, and individualism was thought to be a feature of modern societies. Mauss himself was careful not to slip into a crude evolutionism, but much anthropological writing remains fascinated by the problem of individualism, and by the question of whether or not it is, in some sense, the product of modern living. This view, in some attenuated form, could be said to underlie Dumont's writings on India (1986). However, a slightly different strand of anthropological thinking has sought to emphasize that while persons in some societies might be thought of as inseparable from other persons, this does not mean that individuals do not exist or that people's actions are not evaluated in terms of an individual life trajectory or career. Meyer Fortes made this sort of argument for the Tallensi (Fortes, 1973).[5] What is interesting about this debate in anthropology is that it betrays an anxiety about whether persons who are not separate from other persons or who are defined in relation to other persons can be said to have the appropriate capacities for agency and intention. The western folk model that underpins anthropological theorizing is, in fact, much indebted to psychoanalysis and thus has difficulty in conceiving that an adult person who is not separate from other persons could be capable of agency and intention. Hence the necessity to insist, for example, that the Tallensi are individuals, even if they are bound into a 'web of kinship' to the extent that they do not conceive of themselves as separate persons.

The second point concerns the relationship between identity, self-identity and physical embodiment. Once again, the western folk model underlying anthropological theorizing does not accommodate itself easily to the suggestion that the body is not always the source and locus of identity, and that the interior self is not necessarily the source or locus of intention or agency. The idea of persons as divisible, partible and unbounded has now gained a certain acceptance in the discipline (see, for example, Marriott, 1976, and Strathern, 1988), but there is still considerable resistance to any suggestion that the body might not be the source of identity, or that experience (both of self and of the world) is not always possessed by or located in an interior self.

Thus, one of the points to emerge from a review of anthropological writings on local concepts of the person and the self is that ethnographic data could quite easily be used to support the poststructuralist and deconstructionist critique of the Cartesian cogito. It is evident that the western transcendental subject and the western concept of the person are far from universal, and that while self-awareness may be a universal human attribute, this is not the same thing as saying that everyone has a phenomenological or conceptual category of the person/self which corresponds to western concepts. The variation which exists in the understanding, definition and experience of the self, and in the self's relations with other selves and with the world, does not make the individuals concerned incapable of agency or intention. The anxiety, shared by some feminists and anthropologists, that post-structuralist and post-modernist views of the subject could prove pathologizing may very well be justified politically, but it is not so easy to justify theoretically. It would seem that the only reason why alternative concepts of the person and self appear so threatening is that they challenge western folk models of the person/self, and thus undermine knowledge claims based on subject–object dualisms and the transcendental nature of the knowing subject.

However, cross-cultural variability is not the only issue. A more serious difficulty is raised by the existence of multiple models and/or discourses within cultures, societies, groups or sets of people. Anthropologists have only recently begun to discuss and to document the existence of multiple models, and to look at the variation which exists within cultures as well as between them (see chapter 1 with regard to gender models). This development, which has clear origins in the rise of feminist and Marxist anthropology, has forced a certain re-evaluation of the concept of culture. The result is that anthropologists are more aware than ever that it is impossible to speak of a particular culture as having one model of the person or one conception of the self. What seems evident is that although multiple discourses exist, some discourses are dominant over others and some are appropriate only to specific contexts (see chapter 3). In the case of discourses on the person/self, what appear as dominant models may actually turn out to be relatively divorced from everyday life and experience.

Anthropologists have only recently started to critically reflect upon so-called western models, and they usually do so without bothering to discuss the way in which such models have changed over time, or the ways in which they differ between the groups or sets of people who make up the category 'western' and who are supposed to possess these models. Models of the person and the self are no exception, and when we come to discuss cross-cultural data and the comparative basis on which that data is being presented, we need to ask ourselves where the anthropologists get their models from. The main source is, of course, psychoanalytic theory, and contemporary anthropology draws widely on developmental theory, object-relations theory, ego psychology and the work of Freud and Klein. It very rarely utilizes any Lacanian or post-Lacanian theory, nor any feminist theory. Professional discourses of this kind interact in very complex ways with popular cultural discourses. The result is a set of refractory and resonating models, which find specific and changing emphasis according to the particular social and cultural context in which they are prevalent. Such models utilize specific concepts, but there is much debate about the meaning and the significance of the concepts in both academic and popular discourses. Thus, when anthropologists come to talk about western models of the person and the self, they are referring to a generalized model or set of models which are an amalgam of academic and popular discourses. The important point here is that both academic and popular discourses are mutually informing.

For example, the dominant model of the person/self in western Europe could be said to be one which characterizes the individual as rational, autonomous and unitary. This individual is the author of their own experience and of their knowledge of the world, and their existence is enshrined in post-Enlightenment philosophy, in political theory and in legislation. However, this model of the person/self, which would be accessible through anthropological analysis, has a very complex relationship with the everyday experiences and practices of women and men in Europe. Many people, I would venture to suggest, have occasions when they find it extremely difficult to conceive of themselves as rational, autonomous and unitary. Western European culture has evolved a number of ways (many of them connected to religious belief as well as to popular psychoanalysis) to deal with the fact that individuals do not necessarily experience themselves as the authors of their own experience and of their knowledge of the world. As a result many alternative discourses on the person/self exist, some of them more formalized than others, some of them developed in explicit contra-distinction to the dominant model. The task for anthropologists is to investigate how their own popular discourses or folk models inform the academic discourses which they have at their disposal, and to examine how dominant models relate to alternative popular discourses in the societies they study. I take this theme up with regard to anthropological writing in chapter 7.

Gender and identity

This task is a particularly important one when it comes to the anthropological study of gender because in many cases, including several western cultures, concepts of the person and the self are connected to models for explaining gender difference.[6] The point needs emphasis because of the way in which it is assumed in much anthropological writing that concepts of the person and the self are gender neutral – an assumption that seems to be based on the premise that the person and the self are ontologically prior to gender identity, that is, to the gendered self.

This interesting view contains a number of further premises. One is the idea common in western social science and philosophy that the person is to be understood as an entity that has ontological priority over the various roles and activities through which it engages in social practices and comes to have social meaning and significance. The idea logically presupposes an essence at the core of the person which exists prior to the person's insertion into a social matrix and which is fixed over time. Within philosophical discourse, the question of what constitutes personal identity focuses on the question of what establishes the continuity or self-identity of the person over time. It would not be appropriate to enter into these debates here, but in terms of anthropological discourse it seems quite evident that the most important characteristic of the person over time, and the one which constitutes its identity, is the fact of physical embodiment. This assumption, which is very prevalent in anthropological writing and which is often implicit rather than explicit, is certainly part of a western discourse, rather than a natural fact of human existence. The earlier review of indigenous concepts of the person and the self cast doubt on the assumption that persons are necessarily conceived of as bounded entities with fixed essences, and it questioned the assumption that the body is always the source and locus of identity. This does not mean, of course, that the fact of embodiment is unimportant, but it does mean that it cannot be unproblematically taken as the logical or defining feature of the person or of personal identity through time. Attributes of personhood, such as the continuity and coherence of the person through time, are socially and culturally established, they are not merely given in the physical fact of embodiment. Self-identity is thus something that has to be established socially through a set of discourses which are both discursive and practical. These discourses establish the grounds for identity and the framework(s) within which identity becomes intelligible.

As Judith Butler has pointed out in her discussion of these arguments (1990: 16–17), it is clear that within western cultural discourses ideas about gender identity form a crucial part of the framework within which self-identity becomes intelligible. This is very much as we should expect, given that psychoanalytic discourse provides us with a model for the acquisition of human identity and subjectivity which is crucially dependent on binary sexual difference. While certain philosophical discourses may give ontological primacy to the person and the self *vis-à-vis* gender identity, it is quite apparent that in psychoanalytic and popular discourse the person and the self are not considered as gender neutral. When discourses on the person and the self are approached via discourses on gender, the ontological status of gender in western discourse becomes apparent. Gender identity is manifestly the essence at the core of personal identity in many western discourses. Much contemporary feminist theorizing, for example, employs such an assumption about the ontological status of gender (see chapter 1).

The ontological status of gender in terms of western discourses on the person and the self is reinforced by the assumption that physical embodiment is the logical and defining feature of the person and of personal identity through time. The elision between gender identity and physical embodiment accounts for the extraordinary emphasis in western discourse on the sexually differentiated nature of the human body. The argument that the binary characterization of gender is self-evident because there are two clearly differentiated and natural categories of the body provides the basis for the grounding of gender differences in the biologically given facts of sex. Feminist theory in the social sciences has striven, in the last twenty years, to separate sex from gender and to demonstrate that gender is a social construction, not given in biology or in nature. One very common and simple response to this feminist strategy has been that women and men have biological functions and that it is impossible to escape the fact that human societies need to reproduce. What is curious about this riposte is that it is an extraordinarily weak one, but it is considered by those who reproduce it to be particularly strong. It appears strong, of course, because it is securely grounded within the dominant, naturalized and self-evident discourse regarding gender identity and embodiment. As Yanagisako and Collier (1987) point out, while the feminist strategy of separating sex from gender appears to challenge dominant western models, it actually serves to reproduce the very same assumptions on which those models are based. As I argued in chapter 1 the separation of sex from gender reinforces the idea that there are two clearly differentiated and natural categories of the body. The result is that while the meanings attributed to women and men in any culture may be variable, there is never any doubt that gender is on the body, and the evidence for this is the very fact of sexual differentiation.

The ideas that gender is in the body and that gender has an ontological status which defines the parameters within which personal identity becomes intelligible cannot be considered to be universally applicable. If we turn to look at non-western views of gender difference and the role such difference plays in framing or determining personal identity, we see that gender is often held to have an ontological status, but that its relationship to the question of embodiment is thought to be rather different. Deborah Gewertz discusses Tchambuli views of gender difference, embodiment and personal identity. She observes that her participation in meetings in the men's house led to her being characterized as 'probably not a woman at all, but a strange creature who grew male genitals upon donning trousers'. Her husband was thought to be a feminized male and her daughter was considered to have been purchased from a stranger who needed money (Gewertz, 1984: 618). This redefinition did not affect Gewertz's status as an individual, but it did effectively render her a non-person. To be a person among the Tchambuli is to be a member of a patriclan and, through the possession of certain names, inherited both from the person's patrilineal ancestors and from his or her father's affines, to become the repository of both patrilineal and matrilineal relationships. The definition of personhood among the Tchambuli is, therefore, based on the embodiment of these relationships. As an hermaphroditic woman, Gewertz was effectively self-contained, with neither affines nor kin. She was unable to produce children whose kin would have to be compensated, and thus she was a non-person (Gewertz, 1984: 619).

There are several interesting points to be made about the situation Gewertz describes. First, the Tchambuli conception of the relationship between gender and embodiment is somewhat different from that which pertains under the so-called western model, although there are also some similarities. Gender is certainly located in the body in some sense, because the performance of male activities gives rise to the presumption that this involves the acquisition of male genitals. The issue here is not whether the Tchambuli do or do not think that Gewertz really acquired male genitals. What is important is that gender identity is given as much by the performance of appropriate activities as it is by the possession of the appropriate genitalia. Secondly, there is the question of whether gender identity can be seen as the essence at the core of personal identity. In one sense this would certainly seem to be the case, because becoming classed as an hermaphrodite apparently rendered Gewertz a non-person. However, the crucial point is not that she was of indeterminate gender, but that being sexually complete made her incapable of social reproduction – the production of babies being the vehicle for the reproduction of social relationships. This is connected to a third point about what guarantees the identity or self-identity of a person over time. In this example it seems that identity is guaranteed by a matrix of social relationships rather than by anything which might be deemed an essential attribute of the individual.

Recent ethnography has produced evidence of a large number of cases where it is the performance of particular kinds of activities or tasks which guarantees gender identity rather than simply the possession of the appropriate genitalia. This is the argument, for example, that Harriet Whitehead has made for the Berdache of North America, and that Jane Atkinson makes for the Wana of Indonesia (H. Whitehead, 1981; Atkinson, 1990). These findings stress the importance given in many indigenous models to performance in the determination of gender identity rather than to arguments about essential attributes. In such models physical characterisitics are the sign or effect of sexual difference rather than the cause of gender identity. It is for this reason that if you are a woman who behaves like a man, then you must grow a penis (Gewertz, 1984: 619; Atkinson, 1990: 88–93). In fact, of course, a certain discourse on the relationship between performance or social enactment and gender identity exists in western cultures. It is just that this discourse is, by and large, subordinate to the dominant discourse which stresses the essential and embodied nature of gender identity.

There are a number of other non-western views of gender difference that stress the ontological status of gender, but do so in a way
which questions the relationship between gender and embodiment
established in western discourse. A number of indigenous procreation beliefs and anatomical theories involve ideas about
gendered substances and the multiply gendered nature of human
bodies, as in the Hua case discussed in chapter 1. Models of this
kind stress the ontological status of gender, but they also stress
that gender differences exist within bodies rather than simply or
solely between them (Moore, 1993a). Thus, persons are multiply
gendered, and a model – like the one provided by anthropology –
which stresses that the body can be divided into two naturally
occurring and mutually exclusive categories cannot hope to explain
the relationship between gender and embodiment which these
theories propose.

Ethnographic findings, therefore, question a number of assumptions implicit in dominant western discourses about the relationship between personhood, gender identity and embodiment. In
particular, they question the notion of a single, undisputed and
fixed gender at the core of the person. One immediate difficulty
with ethnographic material on such issues as personhood and gender identity is that it is unclear what the relationship might be
between cultural theories about sexual substances and the actual
experience of being a gendered individual in a particular society.
There is a clear potential discrepancy – as discussed earlier – between a discourse or set of discourses which is culturally available
and the individual experience, interpretation and understanding of
those discourses. However, as discussed by a number of theorists,
there is no meaning to being a gendered self outside the set of
culturally available discourses within which being a gendered self
finds meaning. This does not imply, of course, that individuals are
unable to resist or disagree with cultural discourses. They clearly
are able to do this. But even moments of resistance are moments of
compliance, and discourses which conflict are often constituted in
contra-distinction to each other. It therefore follows that the experience of being a gendered self in a context where gender differences
are thought to lie as much within bodies as between them, and
where aspects of one's gender identity are thought to be fluid and
changeable, is likely to be significantly different from the experience
of being a gendered self in a context which stresses the fixed

and mutually exclusive nature of binary gender categories (see chapter 1).

It seems quite implausible to suggest that psychic development is not affected by these very different ideas about the relationship of individuals to themselves, to others and to their world. This seems crucially important given that the development of self-awareness involves relations with others (that is, intersubjectivity), as well as language. Without these two things the development of self-aware- ness would be impossible. The development of the self and of self- awareness is thus both discursively and practically produced. The particular force of cultural discourses, of course, is that they have material effects, that is they are practically or performatively, as well as discursively, maintained (Bourdieu, 1977, 1990c; see chapter 4 of this volume).

Anthropologists have been very reluctant, until recently, to dis- cuss either the development of self-identity or the development of gender identity. The reasons for this have clearly been both techni- cal and theoretical, though anthropologists have frequently pre- ferred to present the difficulty solely as a technical problem: 'we cannot get inside the heads of actors'. This representation is quite misleading. In fact, the overwhelming difficulty is one of under- theorization, and could be directly addressed by the development both of a theory of the subject and of a theory of the acquisition of subjectivity. In so far as anthropologists have discussed the ac- quisition of subjectivity and gender identity, they have tended to base their work on a straightforward theory of socialization. Socialization has been seen to be effected largely through child- rearing practices or through ritual activities, such as initiation. Work in this area has frequently been very functionalist, especially in the past, in that it tended to imply a situation in which society had need of particular sorts of acculturated persons, who were rather uncomplicatedly female or male. Gender identity was certainly thought to be culturally constructed, but it was conceived of, in the end, as little more than a self-evident outcome of sexual differen- tiation. The theoretical underpinnings of this work tended to be a rather crude Freudianism mixed with object-relations theory and some developmental psychology. Recent work in the discipline is much more sensitive to issues of gender identity, but much of it focuses on pre-Oedipal dynamics and the repudiation of initial maternal attachment by male children (Herdt, 1982, 1984), and there is, as yet, very little cross-cultural work on female children and pre-Oedipal dynamics.

Psychoanalysis, language and subjectivity

Psychoanalysis has provided the humanities and the social sciences with an influential set of theories about the acquisition of subjectivity and gender identity. These theories have been exceedingly controversial, but they have proved persuasive because of the way in which they stress that feminine and masculine identities are not natural or given in biology, but must be constructed and should be understood therefore as cultural achievements. There has been considerable debate amongst feminist scholars as to whether or not Freud's account of the production of sexuality should be seen as an attempt to theorize gender identity on the basis of fixed psychosexual structures which have a single cause (such as the Oedipus complex). One of the issues at stake here is whether or not Freud's theory endorses patriarchal forms of heterosexuality, in the context of a theory of fixed sexual difference which postulates masculinity as the norm (for example, Mitchell, 1974; Mitchell and Rose, 1982; Rose, 1986).

More recently, a number of scholars have drawn on Lacan's rereading of Freud and on various post-Lacanian theories. These theories are attractive because they emphasize the crucial role which language plays in the construction of personal identity. Lacan's theory of the constitution of the subject in language explicitly questions previously dominant notions of the subject in philosophy, sociology and psychology. Lacan argues that the constitution of self is bound up with the world of images and representations and thus the self has no essential qualities, since it is not born, but made. A key point in the construction of the Lacanian subject is the mirror stage. This stage is an account of the primal separation of mother and child, and marks the child's entry into what Lacan calls the Imaginary order, as well as laying the foundations for social and linguistic identity. The mirror stage, which takes place between six and eighteen months, begins with the child's recognition of its image in a mirror. The child identifies with the image and internalizes it. The internalized image or imago provides the child with a sense of wholeness and completeness, and it intro-

duces the child to an idea of its separateness from others. But this
sense of wholeness is illusory, because it conflicts with the child's
fragmented and fragmentary experience of its body (Lacan, 1977: 4–
5). This fragmentation is the result of the fact that different parts of
the body mature at different rates. Furthermore, Lacan is at pains to
emphasize that the self is always a split self, and it must logically be
so because it is based on a relationship between ego and alter-ego.
Lacan argues that the subject, to be a subject at all, must internalize
otherness as a condition of its possibility. It is by identifying and
incorporating the image of itself, which is also the image of another,
that the child begins to represent itself to itself. The result of this is
that while the ego sees itself as its unified image, it is in fact split,
internally divided between self and other (Lacan, 1977: ch. 1).

   In developing this account of the mirror stage Lacan is emphasizing that the ego is not self-contained and autonomous, but is
intersubjective and depends on its relations with the other. He
argues further that the ego is dominated not by reality, but rather by
representation and modes of identification. The result is a subject
which takes itself as its own object and which remains split. Thus
Lacan disputes the assumption of a fixed, unified and naturally
given identity at the core of the subject, while arguing that the
subject's capacity to know itself and know the world is dominated
not by reality, but by the ego's investment in certain images and
representations (Grosz, 1990: 48).

   Lacan's account of the mirror stage also raises interesting questions regarding the relationship between embodiment and identity.
The notion that the formation of the ego is related to a recognition
of the bodily image of another, which is also an image of itself,
clearly means that the formation of the ego is directly linked to an
image of the body's surface. It is by recognizing this body-image
that the subject distinguishes itself from its world. This body is not
simply a physical body, but a 'lived anatomy' and one regulated by
social, symbolic and cultural significations (Grosz, 1990: 43–4). It is
a psychic map of the body, an 'imaginary anatomy', and, as discussed in chapter 1, it varies with different cultural ideas about the
body and biology.

   It is quite clear that Lacan's theory of the subject and of the
relationship between identity and embodiment seems potentially
much more appropriate for understanding non-western views of
the self, like those discussed earlier, than the conventional realist

interpretations of Freud. But perhaps the most valuable part of Lacan's theory for anthropologists is concerned with language, and with the importance of systems of meaning and signification for the constitution of subjectivity. Lacan's account of the child's entry into language involves the passage from the Imaginary order to the Symbolic. Lacan regards the mirror stage and the Imaginary order as sexually undifferentiated; the child's acquisition of a sexual identity occurs only with its entry into the Symbolic. Entry into the Symbolic order is necessary for development and growth, because left alone the mother–child relation would provide an enclosed, circular relation which would make relations with a third (that is, social relations) impossible (Grosz, 1990: 50). According to Lacan, a third term is necessary for social, linguistic and economic exchange to take place (Grosz, 1990: 67). This third term is the Symbolic father, representing the law prohibiting incest. The Oedipus complex is the point at which this third term intervenes in the mother–child dyad, and the child acquires a sexual identity through the repudiation of the mother as love object and acquiescence to the law of the father. As a result of the Oedipalization process, the child acquires a speaking position, a place in culture.

In summary, the positive aspects of Lacan's work for anthropology, as for many other intellectual domains, inheres in his sociolinguistic theory of subjectivity, which enables female and male subjects to be seen as the product of social, historical and cultural systems of signification rather than as biological entities. His theory of the symbolic emphasizes that language, law and symbolic exchange are at the basis of society and social order. Finally, his emphasis on a subject defined by and in language reverses the causal relationship which social science, including anthropology, habitually poses between subjectivity and language. Instead of a subject which speaks, and which is the source and author of meaning and discourse, Lacan proposes a subject which is articulated by language itself, and is the site of representations, inscriptions and meanings (Grosz, 1990: 148).

However, Lacan's theories also pose a number of obvious problems for anthropologists. The privileged signifier of the Symbolic order is the phallus, and sexual difference is constituted with reference to this key signifier (see chapter 1). Thus, feminine and masculine positions, 'being' and 'having' the phallus, are the product not of biology, but of the system of significations, that is, of language. The phallus, as a signifier, is an element of language, which circulates within the system of significations and should not be confused with the penis (Lacan, 1977: 289–90). Lacan's positioning of the phallus as the guarantor of meaning and as the crucial signifier which represents the distinction between the sexes has led to a heated debate about whether or not Lacan's theory is phallocentric (Gallop, 1982; Irigaray, 1985; Ragland-Sullivan, 1986; Mitchell and Rose, 1982). The charges of phallocentrism certainly seem justified on several counts, and it is the phallocentric nature of the theory which opens it to criticism from an anthropological perspective.

Lacanian theory, like psychoanalytic theory in general, postulates a narrative of the acquisition of sexuality and subjectivity which rests on the presumption of a fixed psycho-sexual order. This is clearly the case, in spite of protestations to the contrary by several researchers, since Lacan proposes universal structures and processes within which individuals acquire sexuality and subjectivity, even though both are precarious and constantly threatened by the return of the repressed. Furthermore, the fact that gendered subjectivity is brought about by a fixed set of structures and processes means that all existing social relations must themselves be read in terms of those structures and processes (Weedon, 1987: 56). Such an attempt to lay down the universal conditions for culture itself poses real difficulties from an anthropological point of view.[7]

One of the major obstacles for a feminist anthropology is that Lacan provides no convincing account as to why the phallus should be the key signifier of the Symbolic order, nor why it should stand as the mark of sexual difference. There is also no reason why the law of the father, to which Lacan refers, should be universal. In fact, it seems more sensible to assume that this law is open to cultural reformulation. This is most evident when we turn to look at alternative conceptions of gender and gender identity. Lacan, like Freud, assumes that the assumption of a sexed subject position is only possible in terms of a fixed binarism – to 'be' or to 'have' the phallus. Not only is there no reason why the phallus should everywhere and always be the key signifier of sexual difference, but nor is there any reason to suppose that sexual difference should always and everywhere be constructed in terms of a binary relation between two mutually exclusive categories (see chapter 1). If we assume that local discourses on gender and gender identity make a difference to

the way in which people think about and experience the acquisition
of subjectivity and gender identity, then we cannot afford to assume
that binary exclusivity modelled on external genitalia necessarily
provides an appropriate model for understanding sexual difference
and gender identity around the world.[8]

Lacan and cross-cultural analysis

In terms of the application of Lacanian ideas to ethnographic data
there is as yet very little to go on. There are certainly a large number
of societies which emphasize the importance of detaching male
children from their mothers and from the world of women, which is
often seen as pre-social in some sense. There are many instances in
the ethnographic record of societies which associate identity and
sociality with language and language use. However, to make anything of these generalities much more systematic work would need
to be done.

Amelia Bell is one anthropologist who has investigated the links
between subjectivity, gender and language among the Creek
Indians of north-eastern Oklahoma. Her findings are suggestive.
She notes that for Creeks, language originates in a baby without
form or shape and flows in babbles. In this state, language is referred to as female. When a child is born, it is said to know everything because 'it is still connected to the female "watery
fundament" before birth, in which universal knowledge exists'.
Until the child talks, it is carried by women because 'it has no
bones'. When it starts to speak coherently, it is said to have bones
and must walk by itself (Bell, 1990: 338). The act of speaking forces
an initial separation between child and mother. According to Bell,
Creek babies of both sexes are said to be female because they lack
bones and, by metaphorical extension, the phallus. Through Creek
myths which emphasize the role of a male definitional power in
separating and defining a primordial, generative power which is
female, and through ideas which associate social reproduction with
the male ability to arrest and define the flow of uncontrolled female
productivity, a notion of a male signifier which marks the transition
from an undifferentiated to a differentiated state emerges. Self-
identity and gender identity are associated with the acquisition of
speech and with the entrance into a sociocultural and linguistic
order which is defined by the phallus.

Bell elaborates on this point by making it clear that self-identity and gender identity are constructed in discourse, not only through local ideas about gender relations, social reproduction and the nature of people's relation to the world, but also through various practical activities. Such activities include gender differentiated tasks whose successful performance is thought to be connected to the essential nature of particular sorts of gendered persons. For example, the skill of good cooking is thought to inhere in a woman, and a woman who cannot cook is thought to have been afflicted by 'bad medicine' (Bell, 1990: 335). But the most important activity is speech itself. Creek women and men have a different relationship to language and to language use. Women's speech is typified as flowing and uncontrolled, and women do not speak in most public and ritual contexts. Women apparently 'freely assent to withhold their speech in these public contexts as a sign that they are not dangerous', that their generative capacities are defined and under control (Bell, 1990: 338).

Considered in the light of Lacanian theories of the construction of the subject and of subjectivity, Bell's ethnography is certainly stimulating. However, it cannot be said to prove or disprove Lacan's ideas. Lacan's theory and Bell's ethnography are probably best considered as parallel discourses on subjectivity and gender identity which give mutual insight into each other. Lacanian theory is another folk model, another example of a local philosophy, and its strength resides not in its universal pretensions, but in the specifics of its structure and assumptions.[9] Laying this theory alongside other local philosophies, such as those provided by the Creek or the Hua, is one way of approaching a form of anthropological dialogue. Bringing different models or philosophies close to each other, and maintaining them in a productive tension where one may not clamour louder than the other, is what anthropological interpretation should be all about. There is also an evident intellectual and political imperative in demonstrating the degree to which much social science theory (including psychoanalysis) consists of ontologizing local norms, call them western if you will, so as to provide them with universal application.

Part of the difficulty in applying Lacanian ideas to ethnographic material concerns the question of what is meant by saying that the subject is constituted in language. Lacan is clear on this point and emphasizes that when he says language he does not mean social discourse, he means a system of signification, a system of differences. Lacan is able to maintain this position because although his theory is a theory of the social constitution of the subject, it is not a theory which takes account of social institutions, social practices, local power relations and social discourses. The Lacanian subject is an abstracted, if not actually an abstract, subject, and should not be confused either with the person or with the self (P. Smith, 1988: ch. 5). The assumption of a sexed subject position for Lacan is a prerequisite for agency and for self-identity, but it is not a description of the individual or self, and subjectivity is best understood as an attribute of the self. It is for this reason that Lacanian theory ultimately gives us very little insight into the experience of being a gendered individual in any culture. To understand that experience, it would be necessary to link Lacanian ideas about the constitution of subjectivity to social discourses and discursive practices. This involves linking the assumption of a sexed subject position to all the potential sexed subject positions which are available in social life and social practice. It matters, therefore, that people have local views of the person, of the sort of people women and men are meant to be, of the nature of the biological make-up of the physical being, of the relations between the human and non-human worlds and many other local theories, and are able to use these ideas to reflect on the nature of their experience and on the kind of person/self they believe themselves to be. The assumption of a sexed subject position only makes sense in the context of social discourses and discursive practices; without this context there would be no potential or necessity for any sort of subject, precarious or otherwise.

Recent feminist theory has sought to make use of Lacanian ideas in precisely this way, and to utilize the concept of the non-essentialist subject constituted in language to try to come to grips with individuals' experiences of being a gendered subject (Fuss, 1989: ch. 2). The important point here is to examine how we are all subject to discourse and to the various subject positions which are opened up to us in discourse. Such subject positions can be resisted, both consciously and unconsciously, but it is in terms of these positions, even if in contradiction to them, that we construct a sense of ourselves as selves, as individuals and as persons.

3

FANTASIES OF POWER
AND FANTASIES OF IDENTITY:
GENDER, RACE AND VIOLENCE

Gender identity is both constructed and lived. A point easy enough to make, but very difficult to develop analytically or to know how to act on politically. The issue is one, of course, about the relationship between structure and praxis, between the individual and the social. Much of contemporary social theory addresses this issue, and notable theorists like Anthony Giddens (1979, 1984) have sought to elaborate a theory of agency that would account both for institutionalization and for social change. Pierre Bourdieu's writing (1977, 1990c) works over the same theme, but from a different perspective (see chapter 5). With gender and with race, and with all of that we might term the structuring principles of human social life, the problem of how individuals lead collective lives emerges and re-emerges as one of the most urgent problematics for contemporary social science. Since the 1960s radical reformulations of the notions of the social and the cultural have provided the impetus for a rethinking of the place of the individual and/or subject within structures of power and domination.[1] One important theme has been that of resistance and another, by implication but less often referred to directly, that of complicity. As types of agency, resistance and complicity are notoriously difficult to analyse. What makes individuals resist or comply? It has become increasingly clear that one cannot answer such a question in purely social terms. Issues of desire, identification, fantasy and fear all have to be addressed. Each individual has a personal history and it is in the intersection of this history with collective situations, discourses and identities that the problematic relationship between structure and praxis, and between the social and the individual, resides. Thus, resistance and complicity are not only types of agency, they are also forms or aspects of subjectivity; and as types of agency and as forms of subjectivity they are marked through with structures of difference based on gender, race, ethnicity and so on. There is no comprehensive list of such differences. From an analytical and a political point of view they must be specified in context rather than assumed in advance. At one moment the racial may take priority over the sexual, and in another ethnicity may act as the defining difference. What is clear is that these forms of difference are mutually imbricated, and that although we might talk about priorities or determinations between sets of differences, we should be aware that they can never be truly separate from each other. However, I take as my starting point in this essay the issue of an established link between gender difference and types of agency. My concern is with the relationship between gender identity and gender discourses, between gender as it is lived and gender as it is constructed. At the end of the essay I discuss these issues in the context of interpersonal violence.

An easy way to start a discussion of this relationship is to recall that discourses about sexuality and gender frequently construct women and men as different sorts of individuals or persons. These gendered persons embody different principles of agency – as in the case of many western cultures where male sexuality and persons of the male gender are portrayed as active, aggressive, thrusting and powerful, while female sexuality and persons of the female gender are seen as essentially passive, powerless, submissive and receptive. Such gendered discourses are in all instances constructed through mutual imbrication with the differences of race, class, ethnicity and religion.[2] Thus, individuals, policy makers and institutional and community representatives find it easy to have something of definitive import to say about Muslim men, and white women, and black men and Jewish women, for example. The depressing truth is that few are ever lost for words on such matters of generality and general concern! The intriguing fact about such dominant representations or categorizations is that they have only the most tangential relation to the behaviours, qualities, attributes and self-images of individual women and men. Discourses about gender and gender categories are not powerful because they provide accurate descriptions of social practices and experiences, but rather because, amongst other things, they engender women and men as persons who *are* defined by difference. These forms of difference are the result of the workings of signification and discourse, and when brought into play they give rise to the discursive effects that produce gender difference itself, as well as gender categorizations.

Gender difference, like other forms of difference, is not merely an effect of signification or language. If we accept the view that the concept of the individual or person is only intelligible with reference to a culturally and historically specific set of categories, discourses and practices, then we have to acknowledge the different ways in which the categories 'woman' and 'man', and the discourses which employ those categories, are involved in the production and reproduction of notions of personhood and agency. In addition, such categories and discourses participate in the production and reproduction of engendered subjects who use them to generate both representations and self-representations, as part of the process of constructing themselves as persons and agents. It is for this reason that the symbolic categories 'woman' and 'man', and the difference inscribed within and between them, have something to do with the representations, self-representations and day-to-day practices of individual women and men. But we need some way of theorizing how individuals become engendered subjects; that is, how they come to have representations of themselves as women and men, come to make representations of others and come to organize their social practices in such a way as to reproduce dominant categories, discourses and practices. Reproduction is perhaps more problematic here than resistance, but there are clear difficulties about the relationship to be posited between repression and innovation, between ideologies and interpretations. What is it exactly that dominant categories and discourses determine? At what level do they operate? Do any of us really believe that we identify wholeheartedly with the dominant gender categories of our own societies? It often seems that the problem for anthropologists, as for social scientists in general, is to explain how dominant discourses and categories get reproduced when so few people are prepared to acknowledge that they support or believe in them. Anthropologists and sociologists alike tend to argue that different types of societies, usually calibrated according to some developmental schema, vary in the degree to which they permit dissension, internal critique and innovation. Such distinctions may well be overplayed, but what is clear is that any social theory must account both for the reproduction of dominant categories and discourses and for instances of non-reproduction, resistance and change.

Recent social theory has championed the cause of the knowledgeable actor, one engaged in self-reflection and informed about the conditions of the reproduction of society (for example, Giddens, 1979: 5, 72–3). This positive characterization, however, raises inevitable queries about the types of knowledge such actors are supposed to possess. For the purposes of discussion, we can follow Giddens in identifying at least three: unconscious, practical and discursive. Giddens defines the difference between the practical and discursive forms on the basis of an opposition between 'tacit stocks' of knowledge on the one hand and a type of knowledge that actors can actually express in discourse on the other (1979: 5). This straightforward distinction is, of course, highly problematic, not because there is anything particularly erroneous about Giddens's distinction, but because any distinctions between these forms of knowledge are difficult to sustain. For example, if a stock of knowledge is 'tacit', what is the difference between that and its being unconscious? The notion of 'tacit' is clearly meant to imply that the knowledge is practical rather than intellectual; in other words, it is based on things you know how to do or that have been inculcated into you.

This form of knowledge is exactly that which interests Bourdieu, as well as a number of anthropologists (among them Jackson, 1983), though what distinguishes these writers from Giddens is that they lay more emphasis on bodily experience and on the uses of the body (see chapter 4). Focusing on the body immediately raises the question of how to make a distinction between practical and discursive knowledge. It is easy to take Giddens's point here, but only if we privilege linguistic utterances or textual productions based on visual or written forms. If we focus instead on the strategic execution – as anthropologists so often do – of a series of gestures or practical activities, such as the way in which a particular job gets done, then we must ask ourselves whether such conscious strategization is to be characterized as practical or discursive knowledge.

The fact of the matter is that it is not possible to be fully conscious of what you do with your body even when you have clear intentions in mind; nor indeed with regard to speech utterances, as Freud demonstrated long ago. The practical and the discursive are only free of the unconscious for the purposes of social science analysis. We might argue about the nature of this unconscious – does it, for example, have a universal and invariant form? – but it is equally clear that the unconscious itself is formed through practical and discursive engagement with the world (see chapter 2). Unconscious sources of cognition and praxis are obviously crucial to any notion of agency, and particularly one which would want to take account of salient differences, such as those of gender and race. This means that however crucial the concept of the knowledgeable actor is to an emancipatory social science, we must be wary of positing the actor as superhumanly knowledgeable; that is, we must acknowledge that no one can ever be fully aware of the conditions of their own construction.

Anthropology and the undifferentiated subject

This is particularly important when it comes to a consideration of gender identity as constructed and as lived. We cannot be fully aware of either the unconscious or the social determinants of gender identity, but we can be certain that it is not simply a passive identity acquired through socialization. Identities of all kinds are clearly forged through practical engagement in lives lived, and as such they have both individual and collective dimensions. One of the most difficult sets of processes or relationships to grasp when it comes to a discussion of the construction of engendered subjects is how the social representations of gender affect subjective construc-tions, and how the subjective representation or self-representation of gender affects its social construction. This task has been rendered near impossible in anthropology because the discipline has traditionally worked with collectivities: other cultures. These collectivities are made up of discrete units or individuals. One con-sequence of this position is a very specific view of the nature of the relationship between the social and the individual which stresses that individuals are born into cultures and become members of them through processes of learning and socialization. This implies not only that cultures exist prior to individuals, but that individuals as units exist prior to their contact with the social; that they are somehow singular entities which require a cultural imprint. The weakness of this approach is that it re-creates the individual and the social as antinomies, and is incapable of providing a coherent account of their mutual construction.[3] Since there is no intervening or mediating form, the individual and the social must remain estranged from each other in a shifting series of hierarchical determinations.

This situation is particularly inappropriate for theorizing how people acquire a gender identity, and how they produce and reproduce that identity over time. Until recently, gender identity was completely unproblematic from an anthropological perspective because it was viewed as a direct consequence of exposure to and compliance with cultural categories. In reality, the situation was often very much worse than this because gender identity was frequently assumed to be a straightforward outcome of biological categories, and what was acquired through socialization was really no more than a cultural gloss. Of course, anthropologists were good at handling questions about third genders and other forms of gender difference precisely because they saw them as instances or examples of cultural variation. But this does not alter the fact that the issue of gender identity itself was never seen as a puzzle because it was assumed to be unambiguously determined by cultural categorizations and normative understandings.

Once gender identity is addressed as an enigma, as something that requires explanation, both from a subjective and a collective point of view, it becomes clear that the standard category of individual employed in anthropological writing is inadequate to the task. In spite of the recognition of cross-cultural variability in notions of the individual, person and self (see chapter 2), anthropology habitually deploys a notion of the individual almost completely untouched by recent feminist and post-structuralist critiques of the humanist subject.[4] The terms 'subject' and 'subjectivity' are rarely employed, and the notion of the subject as internally differentiated is largely absent. This essay argues that in order to understand issues of gender identity, both subjectively and socially, anthropology needs a theory of the subject.

The post-structuralist concept of the subject which has emerged from recent debates is quite different from the unified, post-Enlightenment subject which it seeks to deconstruct. The basic premise of post-structuralist thinking on the subject is that discourses and discursive practices provide subject positions, and that individuals take up a variety of subject positions within different discourses.[5] Amongst other things, this means that a single subject can no longer be equated with a single individual. Individuals are multiply constituted subjects, and they can, and do, take up multiple subject positions within a range of discourses and social practices (see chapter 2). Some of these subject positions will be contradictory and will conflict with each other. Thus, the subject in post-structuralist thinking is composed of, or exists as, a set of multiple and contradictory positionings and subjectivities. What holds these multiple subjectivities together so that they constitute agents in the world are such things as the subjective experience of identity, the physical fact of being an embodied subject and the historical continuity of the subject where past subject positions tend to overdetermine present subject positions. The notion of the subject as the site of multiple and potentially contradictory subjectivities is a very useful one. If subjectivity is seen as singular, fixed and coherent, it becomes very difficult to explain how it is that individuals constitute their sense of self – their self-representations as subjects – through several often mutually contradictory subject positions, rather than through one singular subject position.

The reason that anthropology as a discipline has failed to recognize the potential of this approach to the study of gender and gender identity is connected to its overwhelming preoccupation with cultural difference and to the manner in which it has traditionally handled forms of categorical difference. For example, the symbolic analysis of gender in anthropology in the 1970s and 1980s emphasized that gender systems were culturally constructed and therefore variable. This meant, paradoxically, that this important research stressed inter-cultural at the expense of intra-cultural variation (see chapter 1). The implication was that since all cultures defined, constructed and enacted gender in specific ways, each culture had its own distinctive gender system. However, recent work in anthropology has demonstrated that cultures do not have a single model of gender or a single gender system, but rather a multiplicity of discourses on gender which can vary both contextually and biographically (Sanday and Goodenough, 1990; Strathern, 1987). These different discourses on gender are frequently contradictory and conflicting. Anthropology, therefore, has begun to move away from a simplistic model of a single gender system into which individuals must be socialized towards a more complex understanding of the way in which individuals come to take up gendered subject positions through engagement with multiple discourses on gender. This move has enabled researchers to focus on processes of failure, resistance and change in the acquisition of gender identity, as well as instances of compliance, acceptance and investment.

An emphasis on resistance and failure – that is, on the partiality of the effects of discourse – helps to explain the evident disparity between the range of discourses on gender which exist in any particular context and the actual self-representations of individual women and men as engendered subjects. However, this move in anthropology is not as radical as it would at first seem, because issues remain about the *location* of difference. Generally speaking, although anthropology now recognizes the existence of multiple discourses on gender, it still insists on handling them as so many instances of cultural variation within a culture. The notion of the individual has not altered, and nor has the conception of the relationship between the individual/subject and the social. A further intellectual step is required and this involves a recognition of the distinction between locating multiplicity and contradiction between the individual and the ideological/social, and locating such processes and moments of difference within the subject itself. What is necessary is that both levels or moments of difference should be analysed simultaneously; and indeed this is essential since they cannot properly be separated.

It seems evident that individuals do constitute their self-representations as engendered subjects through several different subject positions based on gender. It is equally certain that at different times most individuals will be asked to act out a variety of these subject positions and will have, therefore, to construct themselves and their social practices in terms of a competing set of discourses about what it is to be a woman or a man. These competing notions are not just ideas, because as discourses they have both material and social force. Thus, the enactment of subject positions based on gender provides the conditions for the experience of gender and of gender difference, even as those positions may be resisted or rejected.

Many women acknowledge the feeling of being a different person in different social situations which call for different qualities and modes of femininity. The range of ways of being a woman open to each of us at a particular time is extremely wide but we know or feel we ought to know what is expected of us in particular situations – in romantic encounters, when we are pandering to the boss, when we are dealing with children or posing for fashion photographers. We may embrace these ways of being, these subject positions whole-heartedly, we may reject them outright or we may offer resistance while complying to the letter with what is expected of us. Yet even when we resist a particular subject position and the mode of subjectivity which it brings with it, we do so from the position of an alternative social definition of femininity. (Weedon, 1987: 86)

The experience of gender, of being an engendered subject, is given meaning in discourse and in the practices which those discourses inform. Discourses are structured through difference, and thus women and men take up different subject positions within the same discourse, or rather, the same discourse positions them as subjects in different ways. All the major axes of difference, race, class, ethnicity, sexuality and religion, intersect with gender in ways which proffer a multiplicity of subject positions within any discourse. This notion of the engendered subject as the site of multiple differences, and therefore of multiple subjectivities and competing identities, is the result of the recent feminist critique of post-structuralist and deconstructionist theory. This work has been inspired by Lacan's notion of the subject in contradiction and process, but as De Lauretis points out, the feminist rethinking of the post-structuralist subject – what might be termed the post-post-structuralist subject – is crucially different. In particular, she argues that the notion of identity as multiple and even self-contradictory points to a more useful conception of the subject than the one proposed by neo-Freudian psychoanalysis and post-structuralist theories.

For it is not the fragmented, or intermittent, identity of a subject constructed in division by language alone, an 'I' continually prefigured and preempted in an unchangeable symbolic order. It is neither, in short, the imaginary identity of the individualist, bourgeois subject, which is male and white; nor the 'flickering' of the posthumanist Lacanian subject, which is too nearly white and at best (fe)male. What is emerging in feminist writing is, instead, the concept of a multiple, shifting, and often self-contradictory identity . . . an

identity made up of heterogeneous and heteronomous representations of gender, race and class, and often indeed across languages
and cultures. (De Lauretis, 1986: 9)

This feminist post-post-structuralist view of the subject is, of
course, radically different from the traditional subject of anthropological enquiry, the unitary, whole, rational individual which is
prototypically male. The 'person' in anthropological discourse is
not only male by default, but is also an individual whose identity
is 'externally' guaranteed by difference. Thus, in its unitary nature,
the anthropological individual is defined by difference from other
individuals in the same culture, as well as by its difference from
other individuals in other cultures. The post-post-structuralist subject, on the other hand, is the site of differences; differences which
constitute the subject and are 'internal' to it. This notion of an
'internally' differentiated subject, constituted in and through discourse, is analytically powerful. It is of particular value in analysing
the question of how individuals become engendered and acquire a
gender identity in the context of several co-existent discourses on
gender, which may contradict and conflict with each other. In order
to demonstrate this point, it is necessary to discuss the relationship
between multiple gender discourses and other discourses of difference within a single social setting.

Discourse and domination

Gender discourses are variable cross-culturally. It is clear that many
are oppositional, that is, they are constructed around the idea that
gender has two forms, one female and one male, and that the
categories 'woman' and 'man' which are produced from and
through the various discourses of difference are mutually exclusive.
But not all gender discourses are premised on the mutual exclusivity of the categories 'woman' and 'man'. In many cultures gender
is conceived of processually, and femininity and masculinity are
qualities of biographically located persons rather than categories
(for example, Meigs, 1990; see chapter 2 of this volume). But inter-
cultural variation has to be understood in the context of intra-
cultural variation. The existence of multiple gender discourses
within a single social setting means that in many situations a dis-

course which emphasizes the oppositional and mutually exclusive nature of gender categories can exist alongside other discourses which emphasize the processual, mutable and temporary nature of gender assignment. The co-existence of multiple discourses, however, produces a situation in which the different discourses on gender are hierarchically ordered. This ordering may be both contextually and biographically variable, as well as being subject to historical change. The result is that some discourses overdetermine others, and various sub-dominant discourses develop in opposition to dominant ones.

In many cultures oppositional gender discourses are not only structurally and hierarchically dominant, but also hierarchically stratified internally. As, for example, where woman is seen as man's other, what man is not, the lack and the object of man's desire and knowledge. What is important here is that relations of gender difference are frequently hierarchically ordered both within the dominant discourse and between discourses. This gives rise to a situation in which forms of difference come to stand for each other, and the distinctions encoded between them become the primary site for the production of more general effects of power.

Bob Connell argues for the existence of a number of femininities and masculinities within the same social setting, and he provides several interesting examples from Australian and British life which illustrate the hierarchical relations between dominant and sub-dominant discourses. He describes one Australian school where two identifiable groups of boys are in conflict. One group is the 'Bloods', the traditional, sporting, physically active group who bully the members of the second group known as the 'Cyrils', who are described as 'quite clever little boys who are socially totally inadequate, and yet who have got very good brains. They've all got glasses, short, very fat and that sort of thing' (Connell, 1987: 177). It would be wrong to represent the difference between these masculinities as one of simple choice. For one thing, this pattern of difference, as Connell points out, is a product of the possible subject positions offered to individuals in the school as part of a tension within school policy between success based on sporting achievement and success based on academic excellence. This tension reflects wider social and cultural dynamics about how to succeed in the world, and about what kind of successful masculine self one can be. The school, in order to be attractive to parents and pupils, needs

both kinds of masculinity and rewards both as forms of achievement, albeit in very different ways. However, what is more interesting is the way gender difference is inscribed into this difference
between masculinities. In this case the perpetrators of violence, the
bullies, are the Bloods, and they persecute the Cyrils because of
their effeminacy, their lack of physical prowess and their general
passivity and weakness (Connell, 1987: 177–8).

The inscription of gender difference on to the difference between
or within multiple femininities and masculinities within the same
social setting is of particular interest. One of the things revealed is
the extraordinary variety in the types of social practices, discourses
and institutions which proffer and work over these multiple
femininities and masculinities. The degree to which individuals are
able to recognize the alternative subject positions available to them
is obviously variable, but the lack of any conscious reflection on the
possibility of *choice* does not mean that individuals do not 'select'
from or 'invest' in multiple subject positions (see below). Selection –
and this is clearly a problematic term – is something they can do
through practice, and is not something they have to be consciously
or intellectually aware of (see chapter 4). None the less, the recognition of possible alternative femininities and masculinities is facili-
tated to a certain degree by the fact that competing discourses are
constructed in counterpoint with one another.

Connell provides an example drawn from British advertising, in
which he describes two posters. On one, which is for a perfume, a
woman strides out boldly in trousers, and this image is intended to
depict various things about activity, professionalism, self-determination and so on. In a second poster – and it is worth bearing in
mind how often these posters might occur in the same magazine or
on the same hoarding – a company advertises its sheer stockings,
accompanied by the caption 'For girls who don't want to wear the
trousers' (Connell, 1987: 179). In the case of both posters the images
of femininity they convey are only comprehensible within wider
gender discourses, but their comprehensibility is crucially dependent on the overt reference to the mutually exclusive nature of dominant gender categories. But in the case of the advert for perfume it
is precisely that gap between dominant gender categories and the
actualities of individual women's experience of gender identity and
gender roles which the poster seeks to play with. It is this element of
play which makes the advertisement, and hence the product it

promotes, seductive. The poster which advertises stockings plays with the same gap, but from the opposite perspective, and engages subtly with anxieties about changing definitions of gender roles. In a sense both posters play with each other, interrupt and continue each other's narratives. This parodic play is a noticeable feature of much contemporary advertising. What is interesting about it, of course, is that it continually reinscribes dominant categories and discourses through reference to a fixed relationship of difference, whilst appearing to embody challenge, resistance and change.

It is through engagement with and investment in the subject positions offered by discourses at this level that individual women and men succeed in reproducing the dominant cultural discourse, whilst simultaneously standing at some remove from the categories of that discourse. And it is at this level that we can properly speak of the existence of multiple femininities and masculinities, multiple ways of being feminine or masculine within the same context. However, gender as a form of difference cannot be considered in isolation. The mutual imbrication of sets of salient differences means that one form of difference can be made to stand for another and/or that differences invoked in one context can be used to reformulate differences relevant to another. This is a processual and structural feature of human life which is open to historical change and which always requires careful analytical specification. But a major example in many contemporary contexts is the mutual determination of the discourses on gender and race. A number of scholars have described the way in which the categories of race difference are sexualized, so that men in many oppressed populations are portrayed both as hypermasculine and as feminized.[6] This situation is constantly reinforced by the use of popular metaphors in forms of English that elide oppression with a loss of sexual potency and masculinity: emasculation, castration, impotency. In contexts where race and gender are mutually constitutive of each other it is crucial not to slip into a discussion which implies that gender and race are imbricated only for those who are oppressed or designated as other. Black scholars continually emphasize this point, but it is usually ignored or simply repeated as a form of rhetoric.[7] The dominant experience of gender for white people is one that is deeply racialized, precisely because their race is both an unmarked category and constructed in contra-distinction to other race identities.

However, the mutual imbrication of race and gender so familiar at this historical conjuncture cannot necessarily be superimposed on other contexts. 'Race' and 'gender', as they are used in academic and popular discourse, are generalizing terms with very specific assumptions and structures built in, and as such they are historically and contextually bound notions.[8] A number of writers have argued that in western societies, and perhaps globally, a particular type of hegemonic masculinity orders the structural relationship between alternative femininities and masculinities.[9] This is the masculinity associated with global capitalism and the domination of the West in economic and political life, and it is also the masculinity which constructs the self-representations of those men who actually rule the world – of which, perhaps, the most blatant recent example was Ronald Reagan. Connell (1987) argues that through the workings of this hegemonic form of masculinity the dominant constructions of gender are strongly implicated, if not actually inscribed within, other social relationships. Thus, hegemonic masculinity penetrates political and economic relationships in a way that guarantees that domination itself is gendered (Morgan, 1988). Groups or cabals of powerful heterosexual – that is, represented as heterosexual – men dominate both the running of modern states and relations between states, and they thus control the means of public force and violence. These means are not simply, of course, military, but also economic and political. As a result it is not usually necessary to reinforce their domination through the use of actual physical force, unless – as in the recent Gulf War – there is a breakdown of economic and political control.

It is clear that this hegemonic form of masculinity is accompanied by a hegemonic form of racism. The global structures of power are predicated on racial distinctions which are often used both to overdetermine and to substitute for other forms of difference. The most glaring example in Europe at the present time is the use of the words 'Arab' and 'Muslim' as terms of abuse and categories of discrimination (Kabbani, 1986). The way in which one term substitutes for the other indicates the interpenetration of the various discourses of difference. Likewise, the current treatment of Iraq by the West shows the importance not just of dominating, but of feminizing and pacifying that which is dominated, in order, at least in part, to establish a hierarchical relationship of domination which appears as natural as gender difference itself.

Violence at the national and international level is strongly sexualized, and the distinction between perpetrators and victims of violence is often represented as a genderized difference. Gender, or rather genderized difference, comes to stand for very real differences in power between groups of people and between individuals, and in many contexts is constructed with reference to discourses of racial difference. Gender and race idioms are thus frequently used to order differences in power and/or prestige, with the result that power itself is represented in many contexts as sexualized and racialized.

These forms of hegemonic masculinity and racism are recognizably western; that is, they are connected to the rise of western economic and political power and they are part of a western discourse on otherness. None the less, it is worth pointing out that this particular form of hegemonic masculinity is now global, and it is significant that it has found resonances with a number of local or indigenous masculinities. It is not now possible to analyse discourses on gender, wherever they occur, without recognizing the ways in which they are implicated in larger processes of economic and political change well beyond the control of local communities. The personal experience of gender and gender relations is bound up with power and political relations on a number of different levels. One consequence of this is that fantasies of power are fantasies of identity.

Investing in identity

The discussion in the previous section emphasized that there is no single femininity or masculinity for individual women and men to identify with in their social settings, but a variety of possible femininities and masculinities which are provided by the contradictory and competing discourses which exist, and which produce and are reproduced by social practices and institutions. However, sexuality is intimately connected with power in such a way that power and force are themselves sexualized, that is, they are inscribed with gender difference and with gender hierarchy. This connection does not have to be confined to a discussion of dominant forms of western masculinity or discourses on gender, though it does presuppose the existence of a dominant discourse on gender, which can in theory be a locally specific one. There are two points which arise from this argument. First, femininity and masculinity cannot be taken as singular, fixed features which are exclusively located in women and men. We must agree to this if we recognize that subjectivity is non-unitary and multiple, and that it is the product, amongst other things, of the variable discourses and practices concerning gender and gender difference. Women and men come to have different understandings of themselves as engendered persons because they are differentially positioned with regard to discourses concerning gender and sexuality, and they take up different positions within those discourses.

The advantage of a theory which stresses the existence of competing, potentially contradictory discourses on gender and sexuality rather than a single discourse is that we can ask the question, how is it that people take up a position in one discourse as opposed to another? This question was posed at the beginning of this essay and has not yet been answered. If becoming an engendered person is not just a matter of acquiescing to or identifying with a single femininity or masculinity, then what is it that makes people take up particular subject positions as opposed to others? What accounts for the differences between people with regard to their self-representations as engendered individuals? Why do men differ from each other with regard to their understanding of masculinity, and why do women differ with regard to their understandings and representations of femininity, of what it is to be a woman? What is the relationship between discourses and personal identities?

Wendy Holloway has suggested that we can come to an understanding of what makes people take up certain subject positions by developing a notion of 'investment'. If at any one time there exist several competing, possibly contradictory, discourses on femininity and masculinity, then what motivates individuals to take up one subjective position as opposed to another is their degree of 'investment' in a particular subject position. Holloway conceives of an investment as something between an emotional commitment and a vested interest. (Her use of the term has a strong connotation of cathexis.) Such interest or commitment resides in the relative power, conceived of in terms of the satisfaction, reward or payoff, which a particular subject position promises, but does not necessarily provide (Holloway, 1984: 238). It is clear that the term 'investment' could be problematic here because of its economistic overtones. But it is useful precisely because it allows us to retain a link between questions of power and questions of identity. If we imagine that individuals take up certain subject positions because of the way in which those positions provide pleasure, satisfaction or reward on the individual or personal level, we must also recognize that such individual satisfactions have power and meaning only in the context of various institutionalized discourses and practices, that is, in the context of certain sanctioned modes of subjectivity. Holloway emphasizes the very important point that taking up a position or variety of positions within competing discourses is not just about the construction of self-identity and subjectivity. She argues that to be positioned is always to be positioned in relation to others, and thus, one's interrelations with other individuals – intersubjectivity – will also determine what positions one takes up. In addition, there is the question of the institutional power of dominant or hegemonic discourses, where there are very tangible benefits to be gained from constructing oneself as a particular sort of person and interacting with others in specific sorts of ways. It is important to recognize that investment is a matter not just of emotional satisfaction, but of the very real, material social and economic benefits which are the reward of the senior man, the good wife, the powerful mother or the dutiful daughter in many social situations. It is for this reason that modes of subjectivity and questions of identity are bound up with issues of power, and with the material benefits which may be consequent on the exercise of that power.

It would be a mistake, however, to represent the process of taking up a subject position as one of simple choice. For one thing, the historical contextualization of discourses means that not all subject positions are equal, some positions carry much more social reward than others and some are negatively sanctioned. The role of dominant or hegemonic discourses on gender and gender identity is pivotal here. While non-dominant discourses certainly provide subject positions and modes of subjectivity which might be individually satisfying and which might challenge or resist dominant modes, those individuals who do challenge or resist the dominant discourses on gender and gender identity frequently find that this is at the expense of such things as social power, social approval and even material benefits. The same argument may also explain why those in power are so vulnerable to accusations about their sexuality and sexual behaviour. The second reason why the taking up of a subject position cannot be seen as a matter of choice is linked to the multiple and contradictory nature of subjectivity. The fact that individuals take up multiple subject positions, some of which may contradict each other, obviously cannot be explained in terms of a theory of rational choice. Holloway's notion of investment reminds us of the emotional and subconscious motivations for taking up various subject positions. In this context fantasy, in the sense of ideas about the kind of person one would like to be and the sort of person one would like to be seen to be by others, clearly has a role to play. Such fantasies of identity are linked to fantasies of power and agency in the world. This explains why concepts such as reputation are connected not just to self-representations and social evaluations of self, but to the potential for power and agency which a good reputation proffers. The loss of reputation could mean a loss of livelihood, and the lack of good social standing can render individuals incapable of pursuing various strategies or courses of action. The use of the term 'fantasy' is important here because it emphasizes the often affective and subconscious nature of investment in various subject positions, and in the social strategies necessary to maintain that investment. I want to turn briefly now to a discussion of the relationship between gender identity and interpersonal violence as a way of considering these issues in a more concrete manner.

Gender identity and interpersonal violence

Holloway herself does not discuss the relationship between identity, subjectivity, power and violence. However, it is possible to suggest a link between the thwarting of investments in various subject positions based on gender and interpersonal violence. Thwarting can be understood as the inability to sustain or properly take up a gendered subject position, resulting in a crisis, real or imagined, of self-representation and/or social evaluation. Such crises can be of various degrees of seriousness and of variable duration. Thwarting can also be the result of contradictions arising from the taking up of multiple subject positions, and the pressure of multiple expectations about self-identity or social presentation. It may also come about as the result of other persons refusing to take up or sustain their subject positions *vis-à-vis* oneself and thereby calling one's self-identity into question. A phrase such as 'she/he wasn't a proper wife/husband to me' emphasizes the inter-subjective nature of questions of gender and gender identity. It is equally a phrase which can cover everything from a failure of sexual relations to the failure of economic provisions. Thus, thwarting can characterize the inability to receive the expected satisfactions or rewards from the taking up of a particular gendered subject position or mode of subjectivity. It is, of course, not necessary for an individual to have a specific, conscious view of what the satisfactions or rewards ought to be for them to experience thwarting.

Many writers report that violence is often the outcome of an inability to control other people's sexual behaviour, that is, other people's management of themselves as engendered individuals. This explains violence not only between women and men, but also between mothers and daughters, between sisters-in-law and between men themselves. In all such situations what is crucial is the way in which the behaviour of others threatens the self-representations and social evaluations of oneself. Thus, it is the perpetrator of violence who is threatened and experiences thwarting.

Interestingly enough, many violent events occur in situations where the thwarted party is likely to suffer direct material loss, whether in terms of social status or access to economic resources, as a result of the insufficiencies – so perceived – of the victim of the violence. Once again, fantasies of identity are linked to fantasies of power, which helps to explain why violence is so often the result of a perceived, rather than a real, threat. For example, wives are frequently beaten for imagined infidelities, which makes violence and the threat of violence so much more effective as a means of social control.

Peter Wade's discussion of gender relations and violence in Colombia demonstrates the existence of multiple and contradictory discourses on gender, and the way in which the dominant discourse on gender emphasizes that the differences between women and men are categorical (1994). His article is particularly useful because it shows extremely clearly how the goals of identity and person-hood are different for women and men, and how engaged indivi-duals are in strategies which invest in and maintain particular self-representations and social evaluations. Dominant discourses, and the differential subject positions which those discourses proffer women and men, work to limit the strategies which individuals can pursue. The evident satisfactions and rewards, many of them actually economic, which follow on from the successful management of modes of gendered subjectivity – most particularly for men – are directly demonstrated. The relationship between fantasies of masculine identity and fantasies of power is especially volatile. Men have an investment in two competing discourses, one the providing husband/father and the other the *hombre parrandero*. The fantasy of masculine identity is predicated on the ability to balance these two modes. Men, therefore, have to pursue strategies to get their wives to submit to their interests, with the result that there is often conflict between spouses over the man's extra-domestic commitments. Discourses on gender identity, as Wade points out, structure relations not only with women, but also with other men. To be an *hombre parrandero* is a source of prestige among men, as well as an expression of male solidarity, and whilst participation in *parrandas* certainly establishes close and affective relations with other men, it also provides a man with a crucial economic network. Thus, successful economic strategies involve successful management of gender identity. The volatile relationship between fantasies of identity and fantasies of power frequently gives rise to violence both between women and men and between men. The successful man is one who manages the relationship between the role of husband/father and the *hombre parrandero*, and thus contains and controls his domestic situation, while at the same time keeping up his reputation as a good friend. The crucial point here is representation and others' interpretation of that representation. The perfect husband and the perfect friend do not exist, but their images and effects must be kept constantly in play. In this sense violence, when it occurs, is the result of a crisis of representation, as well as the result of conflict between social strategies which are intimately connected to those modes of representation.

Wade emphasizes that the experience of identity is bound up with the experience of power, and that challenges to the exercise of power or to its effects in terms of status, strategies and interests are perceived as threats to identity. The obverse appears equally true, so that challenges levelled at an individual's gender identity and gender management, specifically as these are reflected in the behaviour of others to whom that individual is closely connected, may be perceived as a threat to power, position, control and even assets.

Penny Harvey (1994) provides two interesting examples. The first is of a woman regularly beaten by her husband, who reported that his behaviour could be attributed to the fact that he was seeing another woman, and that this always makes men vicious towards their wives, especially when their lovers are not really under their control. It was significant in this case that the man's lover was also the lover of one of the local policemen. The second is the example of a woman who was severely beaten by her husband, allegedly for all the faults of his other lovers, calling them by name as he did so. In both cases the violence is potentially explicable, in part, as the thwarting of the expected outcome of particular modes of gendered subjectivity. And, in both cases the self-representations of the individual men as gendered persons included the right and the power to have extra-marital relations as part of a definition of masculinity as active and aggressive, and hierarchically defined in relation to femininity. The wider Andean cultural understanding of complementarity as predicated on hierarchical difference is particularly relevant here, as Harvey points out. However, the ability to pursue extra-marital relations is a consequence of a number of factors: amongst these are gender discourses, gender identities, the hierarchical nature of gender difference and a particular set of gender relations. But the reality of the situation, as the ethnography makes clear, is that in the context of these specific extra-marital relations attributes of desirable masculinity, far from being confirmed, are challenged, perhaps even denied. The men cannot control their lovers as they would wish, they cannot control other men's access to these women and therefore they cannot control the definition of their own masculinity because they cannot control the definition of or the social practices surrounding the femininity of their lovers. The only women they can control are their wives; and it is they who confirm their husbands' masculinity by their proper adoption of the opposite feminine subject position, and so their husbands hit them. Once again violence is the consequence of a crisis in representation, both individual and social. The inability to maintain the fantasy of power triggers a crisis in the fantasy of identity, and violence is a means of resolving this crisis because it acts to reconfirm the nature of a masculinity otherwise denied.

In those social settings where dominant discourses on gender construct the categories 'woman' and 'man' as mutually exclusive and hierarchically related the representation of violence itself is highly sexualized, and is inseparable from the notion of gender and, in particular, from the notion of gender difference. However, gender difference is not the only form of difference employed in the representation of violence. Other forms of difference, notably class and race, are crucial in the formation of discourses on social identity, and are constitutive of modes of subjectivity in the same way as gender. It follows, therefore, that these forms of difference will be strongly implicated in the relationship established between fantasies of power and fantasies of identity. Whenever that relationship is called into question, violence, or the threat of violence, may result. In making this argument I do not want to fall into the trap of suggesting that all violence is of similar origin, and/or that there is no difference between the forms and degrees of violence, or in terms of its incidence. But I do want to suggest that in terms of interpersonal violence, and with regard to the relationship between violence and particular forms of difference – gender, race, class – we might come closer to an understanding of the phenomenon if we shift our gaze and move from imagining violence as a breakdown in the social order – something gone wrong – to seeing it as the sign of a struggle for the maintenance of certain fantasies of identity and power. When we come to a final consideration of the relationship between violence and gender, it is clear that violence of all kinds is engendered in its representation, in the way it is thought about and constituted as a social fact. In its enactment as a social practice it is part of a discourse, albeit a contradictory and fragmented discourse, about gender difference.

4

BODIES ON THE MOVE: GENDER, POWER AND MATERIAL CULTURE

Gender difference and the material world

Bodies take metaphors seriously. The phrase is Bourdieu's (1990c: 71–2), and its suggestive power has much to do with the immediate recognition that we all live our lives through actions performed in structured space and time. The material world that surrounds us is one in which we use our living bodies to give substance to the social distinctions and differences that underpin social relations, symbolic systems, forms of labour and quotidian intimacies. Theories of gender difference – and indeed other forms of difference – frequently give insufficient attention both to bodily praxis as a mode of knowledge and to the material context in which that practice takes place.[1]

The contemporary social sciences now take it as axiomatic that gender is a cultural construct, that, far from being natural objects, women and men are fundamentally cultural constructions. The obvious fact of biological differences between women and men tells us nothing about the general social significance of those differences; and although human societies all over the world recognize biological differences between women and men, what they make of those differences is extraordinarily variable. We cannot deal, therefore, with the observable variability in the cultural constructions of gender across the world or through historical time simply by appealing to the indisputable fact of sexual difference.

This argument is an uncontentious one for many people, but it is none the less easy to lose sight of the analytical consequences of this position because of the way gender ideologies work to appear natural, pre-given and eternal. For example, it is in the natural order of things that men head households; that women are responsible for child care; and that women do not wage war. We find these naturalizations of gender relations made explicit in the material world. The apparently evidential nature of the sexual division of labour is almost everywhere concretized through material objects. The earliest theorizations of the sexual division of labour, like many of those which have followed since, naturalized the differences between women and men through appeal to the material world.

> Division of labour was a pure and simple outgrowth of nature: it existed only between the sexes. The men went to war, hunted, fished, provided the raw material for food and the tools necessary for these pursuits. The women cared for the house, and prepared food and clothing, they cooked, weaved and sewed. Each was master in his or her own field of activity; the men in the forest, the women in the house. Each owned the tools he or she made and used; the men, the weapons and the hunting and fishing tackle, the women the household goods and utensils. (Engels, [1884] 1972: 149)

Thus, the world is divided into gender specific domains and spaces, and into gender specific tasks, and both domains and tasks are associated with particular material items. An established relationship between particular material items and persons of a specific gender seems to be common to societies all over the world, though more elaborated in some as compared to others. This makes it easy to fall into the trap of suggesting that gender specific tasks and domains, with their associated material items, simply reflect the obvious division of the world into women and men. The relationship between gender and material culture remains unproblematic because the material world somehow reflects the appropriate cultural ideas about gender, and also demonstrates in a concrete and practical way the nature of relations between the sexes.

There is something to be said in favour of this 'reflectionist' type of argument, and there was a time when it was very popular in the social sciences and humanities. An anthropological example drawn from Caroline Humphrey's work on the organization of space inside a Mongolian tent makes the point:

> In practice . . . the floor area of the tent was divided into four sections, each of which was valued differently. The area from the door, which faced south, to the fireplace in the centre, was the junior or low-status half, called by the Mongols the 'lower' half. The area at the back of the tent behind the fire was the honorific 'upper' part, named the xoimor. The division was intersected by that of the male or ritually pure half, which was to the left of the door as you entered, and the female impure, or dirty section to the right of the door, up to the xoimor . . . A woman's object was considered to pollute the men's area and a special ceremony might have to be performed to erase this. (1974: 26)

Encoded in this passage, and made explicit in the rest of Humphrey's article, is a series of ideas about how the organization of space reflects the hierarchical nature of relations between women and men. Women are polluting and any object associated with them is also polluting, and the position of such objects within the tent must be controlled and monitored in order to make sure that they do not pass into the ritually pure, male part of the tent. Just as women themselves must be monitored and controlled by men. The divisions discussed by Humphrey also make appeal to a fairly common set of symbolic oppositions which are associated with the female and the male. So that women, or rather 'woman', as a symbolic category is associated with the left, the impure and the lower, while 'man' is associated with the right, the pure and the higher. Symbolic oppositions such as these, which may stand as transformations of or metaphors for each other, are by now the routine products of semiotic or structuralist analyses in the social sciences. The value of working out the inner logic and structural relations between cultural symbols, whilst emphasizing the contextual nature of symbolic meaning, is clear. Structuralist analysis has its place, as both Bourdieu (1977, 1990c) and Ricoeur (see Moore, 1990a) argue, as long as it is recognized that the decoding of symbolic structures does not constitute an interpretation of those structures.

In the traditional social anthropological view cultural beliefs, attitudes and symbols were seen as reflecting primary sets of social relations, and for this reason Humphrey links the hierarchy which apparently exists between the symbolic categories 'woman' and 'man' to the existence of relations of dominance or to particular sets of social relations between women and men. She is not incorrect in doing this, but the complexity of the relationship between cultural symbols or ideologies and specific sets of social relations – that is, between cultural representations and what people really do in their day-to-day lives – defeats any attempt to specify such a relationship as being merely one of reflection. Marxist scholars in a number of disciplines, including social anthropology, tackled this problem by reversing the relationship and arguing that cultural ideologies, far from reflecting social relations, actually serve to distort and mystify them, in order to maintain the status quo through a misrecognition of the sources of power and oppression. Recent critiques, however, have pointed out that what is missing in both the structuralist/ semiotic and Marxist type of analysis is the social actor. Meaning does not inhere in symbols, but must be invested in and interpreted from symbols by acting social beings. Interpretation is the product of a series of associations, convergences and condensations estab- lished through praxis, and not the result of an act of decoding by an observer. This privileging of the interpretations of social actors inevitably results in a series of questions about how to connect individual interpretations with collective discourses or ideologies. How is it that actors construct an understanding of their world, an understanding of themselves as gendered individuals and an understanding of social relations through the dominant cultural ideologies or dominant cultural discourses about gender, whilst at the same time apparently dissenting from those cultural discourses to a significant degree? It is clear that people in a variety of contexts do this, as discussed in the previous chapter. If we take contem- porary British society as an example, it is evident that many women construct themselves as women in ways which do not subscribe to the dominant cultural definitions of womanhood.[2] This point has particular pertinence when we come to consider the relationship between gender and material culture.

If we look at Caroline Humphrey's analysis, we can see that it is assumed that all persons are equally affected by dominant cultural ideologies and symbol systems, and that people's behaviour and/or their social relations will in some sense conform to these dominant representations of gender relations. This assumption has to be there to some extent in structuralist and semiotic analysis in anthropology because the link between cultural ideologies and social relations is supposed to be one of reflection. But I want to return to the problem raised in the previous chapter, and use the medium of material culture to pose again the question of how we theorize the relationship between dominant representations or cultural discourses about gender and what people actually think and do. How is it possible for people both to consent to and dissent from the dominant representations of gender when they are encoded in the material world all around them?

Space, place and interpretation

Pierre Bourdieu was one of the first analysts to try to integrate a structural analysis with what people do, and to try to integrate the self-images or self-representations people build up of themselves with dominant cultural ideologies or world-images, as Bourdieu would term them. He describes the interior of the Kabyle house:

The interior of the Kabyle house, rectangular in shape, is divided into two parts by a low wall: the larger of these two parts, slightly higher than the other, is reserved for human use; the other side, occupied by the animals, has a loft above it. A door with two wings gives access to both rooms. In the upper part is the hearth and facing the door, the weaving loom. The lower, dark, nocturnal part of the house, the place of damp, green or raw objects – water jars set on the benches on either side of the entrance to the stable or against 'the wall of darkness', wood, green fodder – the place too of natural beings – sleep, sex, birth – and also of death, is opposed to the high, light-filled, noble place of humans and in particular of the guest, fire and fire-made objects, the lamp, kitchen utensils, the rifle – the attribute of the manly point of honour (nif) which protects female honour (hurma) – the loom, the symbol of all protection, the place also of the two specifically cultural activities performed within the house, cooking and weaving. The meaning objectified in things or places is fully revealed only in the practices structured according to the same schemes which are organised in relation to them (and vice versa).

The guest to be honoured is invited to sit in front of the loom. The opposite wall is called the wall of darkness . . . a sick person's bed is placed next to it. The washing of the dead takes place at the entrance to the stable. The low dark part is opposed to the upper part as the female to the male. (Bourdieu, 1977: 90)

Bourdieu is making a very familiar argument here, because he explicitly says that the Kabyle house is organized according to a set of oppositions – fire: water, cooked: raw, high: low, light: shade, day: night, male: female – and that these oppositions are all metaphors of each other. However, he goes beyond a standard structuralist analysis, and argues that these symbolic meanings are not inherent in the organization of space, but have to be invoked through the activities of social actors. It is only when you actually place a sick person against the wall of darkness or place an honoured guest in front of the loom that meanings are invoked. And, of course, failure to do such things also has significance, and may serve to confound the expectations of others, and thus potentially revoke or bring into question sedimented cultural meanings and values. Actors are continually involved, therefore, in the strategic interpretation and reinterpretation of the cultural meanings that inform the organization of their world as a consequence of their day-to-day activities in that world.

Bourdieu suggests that for an actor to strategically invoke or revoke certain meanings, it is not necessary for the actor to be involved in conscious, intellectual reasoning about alternative interpretations and strategies, though there will be occasions when this is the case. The ability to pursue alternative strategies within symbolically structured space requires no more than the practical knowledge of how to proceed within that space, of what you should and should not do.

> Adapting a phrase of Proust's, one might say that arms and legs are full of numb imperatives. One could endlessly enumerate the values given body, made body, by the hidden persuasion of an implicit pedagogy which can instil a whole cosmology, through injunctions as insignificant as 'sit up straight' or 'don't hold your knife in your left hand', and inscribe the most fundamental principles of the arbitrary content of a culture in seemingly innocuous details of bearing or physical and verbal manners, so putting them beyond the reach of conscious and implicit statement. (Bourdieu, 1990c: 69)

This process of learning through practical enactment does not mean that actors can never bring these principles to discourse, nor does it mean that they are unable to manipulate meanings and outcomes – they can and do through day-to-day activities.[3] Not all these instances of manipulation will be conscious in the sense of thought-out strategies that can be expressed in language. Bourdieu is frequently charged with having developed a theory that allows little room for agency and/or social change.[4] This is perhaps because his emphasis on the intersection of social location with sets of structuring principles that are embodied through repetition and enactment (habitus) implies that social reproduction and conformity are paramount. In fact, Bourdieu stresses, without providing many concrete examples, that because praxis is itself a moment of interpretation, if not actual manipulation, the role of the actor is crucial to his theory.[5] There is room here both for creativity and for social change because actions themselves can be a type of critical reflection that does not necessarily have to involve conscious, discursive strategizing. When it comes to the question of the body and its enactment of cultural principles, Bourdieu emphasizes that embodiment is a process, and that the body is never finished, never perfectly socialized.

Bourdieu's focus on the relationship between social location and embodiment means that a notion of position and positionality runs through his work. Bourdieu's analysis of power is closely linked to this notion of positionality through a consideration of distinctions based on gender and on class. Bourdieu makes it clear that actors' interpretations of the material world, and the kinds of activities they perform in socially structured space, are governed by their particular position within social relations and dominant cultural discourses. In the case of the Kabyle Bourdieu describes the different positions of women and men with regard to dominant discourses and social relations by concretizing them as a difference in physical perspective:

> One or other of the two systems of oppositions which define the house . . . is brought to the foreground, depending on whether the house is considered from the male point of view or the female point of view: whereas for the man, the house is not so much a place he enters as a place he comes out of, movement inward properly befits the woman. (1977: 91)

Bourdieu's grounding of perspective in the body makes his notion of position rather more physically specific than the feminist notion of a standpoint. Standpoint theory stresses that the positionalities arising from structured inequalities are much more than a perspective because they are institutionalized and collective. However, the two theories are simply using the term perspective in different ways. Bourdieu does recognize structural inequalities and he argues that they give rise to social divisions which produce what he terms the 'habitus', that set of structuring principles and common schemes of perception and conception that generate practices and representations (1990c: 53). In fact, Bourdieu, like feminist standpoint theorists, tends to treat women as a class, thus obscuring differences within the category. But he does recognize that there is a link between the different positions of women and men with regard to dominant cultural values and their self-understandings and self-representations as gendered individuals (1990a).

> The opposition between the centrifugal, male orientation and the centripetal, female orientation, which as we have seen, is the true principle of the organisation of domestic space, is doubtless also the basis of the relationship of each of the sexes to their 'psyche', that is, to their bodies and more precisely to their sexuality. (Bourdieu, 1977: 92)

This is no doubt Bourdieu's concession to a phenomenological view of the body, but its more powerful persuasiveness lies in the link he attempts to establish between the body and knowledge. Praxis is not simply about learning cultural rules by rote, it is about coming to an understanding of social distinctions through your body, and recognizing that your orientation in the world, your intellectual rationalizations, will always be based on that incorporated knowledge. Bourdieu's work contains a method for understanding the pervasive power of symbols and of the social distinctions on which they are based because he reminds us that whether we are actors or analysts we know that symbols are powerful because they do something to our bodies.

Bourdieu appears to hold psychoanalysis in some contempt, and he does not develop a theory of the body that could incorporate a notion of the distinction between conscious and unconscious motivations and actions.[6] Consequently, he does not focus on what happens when these different sets of motivations are in conflict. His strongly socialized and collective view of the body in its relationship to habitus means that he does not adequately theorize individual experiences and motivations. He does acknowledge that social actors have individual trajectories within social locations (fields), and this allows him to incorporate a certain conception of lived personal history, but one that is rather abstract. Bourdieu argues that the singular habitus of members of the same class is united through a series of homologies, and that each is a structural variant of the others. There is, therefore, room for something that Bourdieu terms 'personal style'. He acknowledges also that each individual has a singular trajectory based on a 'series of chronologically ordered determinations that are mutually irreducible to one another' (1990c: 60). He maintains that history is crucial since new experiences are always overdetermined by past ones, but, rather than seeing this as giving rise to distinct experiences for the individual subject, he chooses to emphasize instead that new experiences will be 'dominated by the earliest experiences, of the experiences statistically common to members of the same class' (1990c: 60).[7]

Bourdieu is keen to transcend what he sees as the sterile antinomies of the social sciences, including those between the individual and the collective (1988). His theory of the body is part of this attempt. In his discussion of the sexed body he is particularly concerned to emphasize the relationship between knowledge and recognition that provides the grounds for the apprehension of difference through bodily praxis (1990a: 12). Both emotions and knowledge are embodied forms that can never be brought entirely into discourse. However, his tendency to treat groups as classes makes it extremely difficult for him to specify the consequences of the intersections of sets of different social distinctions for individuals in specific contexts. Like feminist standpoint theory, once questions are raised about differences within the identified categories as opposed to between them – for example, differences between women – then the theory provides little guidance as to how to handle difference. One consequence for Bourdieu is that his concept of positionality is devoid of any notion of a multiple subjectivity constituted through multiple positions.

Bourdieu does raise the question of subjectivity, but he does not develop it theoretically in great detail.[8] The strength of his approach is its insistence on the materiality of subjectivity. This stems, in part, from certain strands of Marxist thinking in his work. He explicitly says that the schemes of perception and conception that form the habitus are derived from the conditions of existence, and particularly from the social divisions of labour.[9] Bourdieu's analysis of cognition and symbolism is not one that floats free from the conditions under which people actually live. This emphasis on the materiality of subjectivity allows Bourdieu to transcend, to a degree, the antinomy between the subjective and the objective, between the individual and the world. His subject is one born of a world of objects, where schemes of perception and thought are inculcated through the activities performed in symbolically structured space and time (1990c: 76). The subject is never separated from the material conditions of its existence, and the world is never free of the representations that construct it:

> the acts of cognition that are implied in misrecognition and recognition are part of social reality and . . . the socially constituted subjectivity that produces them belongs to objective reality. (Bourdieu, 1990c: 122)

Bourdieu sees social structures and cognitive structures as recursively linked, and it is the correspondence between them that provides the foundation for social domination. He discusses these points at length in his work with regard to gender and class, but he gives little space to other forms of difference.[10] His relative inattention to questions of race is surprising given his theory of the body and of bodily praxis.

bell hooks has provided several powerful descriptions of the relationship between space, place and black identity in the United States (1991: chs 5, 10, 15). The differences of race are inscribed in such things as the physical process of leaving the community, crossing the tracks and going to work in white homes. hooks gives several examples of the gendered nature of physical space, emphasizing that houses belonged to women, and that they were sites of identification and resistance (1991: 41–3). These homes provided an alternative space for community and self-valorization removed from the topography of racial oppression and discrimination. Such spaces have to be constructed both imaginatively and physically, but through the way that they are lived bodily practices of incorporated knowledge bind the material and the symbolic indissolubly. hooks gives an account of working as a professional academic in a context where physical space is part of the unmarked category 'white', and where this fact dictates forms of comportment and forms of speech. She describes clear joy at returning to a space constructed in terms of understandings that form part of her sense of self, as when coming home to rest from the rigours of a lecture schedule.

hooks's descriptions of what it means to be a black intellectual are based on clear accounts of the intersections of race, class and gender. The reality of this experience is a series of complex crossings and recrossings. To leave certain spaces and pass into others is to know in your body what the differences of race involve; it is to know oppression and discrimination intimately in a way which does not allow for the separation of the physical from the mental. The powerful symbolism of notions of place, location and positionality in contemporary feminist theory demonstrates just how much we come to know through our bodies, and how much our theorizing is dependent on that knowledge. The multiple nature of subjectivity is experienced physically, through practices which can be simultaneously physical and discursive. Current theories of multiple positionalities and multiple subjectivities are resonant for social analysts who live these contradictory, conflicting and compelling differences.[11]

Language and behaviour: the politics of domination

The most compelling question in any discussion of social domination is one about the possibilities for resistance. If embodied knowledge simply provides a physical form of interpellation as neat and tidy as that proposed by Althusser, then how can we account for resistance, contradiction and change? It seems implausible to suggest that the fit between physical practices and discursive interpretation will always be perfect. Language and behaviour are frequently at odds with one another, as psychoanalysis so amply demonstrates. What can no longer be spoken is repeated in behaviour. It seems clear, then, that body knowledge can both refuse us and traduce us. It can insist on things that we would like to leave behind and it can continue to guide us when we have lost all sense of strategy and purpose.

What emerges from this is that resistance does not need to be discursive, coherent or conscious.[12] The organization of the material world, however conventional and well established, is never complete or finished. The appearance of finality and completeness is a function both of the totalizing view of the analyst and of the nature of dominant value systems and discourses. Bourdieu's insistence on strategies of invocation and revocation, discussed earlier, reminds us that meanings are not static and that they do not inhere in the material world itself. Behaviour, sets of activities conducted in structured space, can be used to 'read against the grain' of dominant discourses, to expose the arbitrary nature of their construction. If one cannot resist by placing oneself outside dominant structures and discourses, one can none the less displace oneself within them. Individuals can refuse the construction of gender as it is presented, they can approach this construction deviously or ironically, they can refer to it endlessly, but do so against its purpose, against the grain.

Much of the difficulty in analysing social domination, power and resistance comes from an uncertainty about key terms. Resistance, for example, normally implies a conscious, coherent strategy. It is possible to extend the term to cover forms of inertia, but analysts usually assume that foot-dragging, go-slows and petty pilfering from employers are conscious strategies. 'When is resistance resistance?' 'When you realize you are doing it.' Much hinges, then, on whether an action is conscious or unconscious. The problem is a routine one and concerns the borderline. A great many actions are unthought and unthought out, unformulated and inchoate, half apprehended and concrete only after their effects are known. They do not come into discourse before their execution, and often not afterwards. But such actions are deliberate, calculated and calculating. They require no more, in those familiar words, than a knowledge of how to proceed. Are such actions really unconscious?

The problem is compounded because certain actions, particularly those involving resistance or possible resistance, can be of an indeterminate nature. It can be very difficult to tell whether someone is just making a mistake or deliberately doing something differently, being careful or going slow.

The issue of interpretation is an important one because it highlights the fact that dominant structures and discourses involve a high degree of indeterminacy.[13] Their very power comes from their generality, from the way in which the broad outlines of the principles of division they encode act as a backdrop against which conflict and contradiction can take place. Dominant discourses of gender, for example, may seem removed from the experiences of individual women, but that very distance means that they are rarely directly challenged by the vagaries of lived experience. 'Just like a woman' is a commonplace phrase in British society which says everything and tells us nothing. As an instance of the dominant discourse on gender, it will never be contradicted by the complexities of individual women's lives.

However, we know that dominant discourses are not impervious to change, and that one of the major ways in which change comes about is through processes of interpretation and reinterpretation (Bourdieu, 1990c: ch. 3). Shifts in meaning can result from a reordering of practical activities. If meaning is given to the organization of space through practice, it follows that small changes in procedure can provide new interpretations of spatial layouts. Such layouts provide potential commentaries on established ways of doing things and divisions of privilege. Shifting the grounds of meaning, reading against the grain, is often something done through practice, that is, through the day-to-day activities that take place within symbolically structured space. This can involve small things, such as putting something in the wrong place or placing it in relation to something else from which it is normally kept separate. It can include using space in a different way or commandeering space for new uses or invading the space of others.

The importance of restructuring the physical relations of the material world in order to resist or combat and then change the conceptual and social relations of gender was clearly recognized by nineteenth-century feminist reformers. These women, who were engaged in campaigns to change relations between women and men, to change women's position within the home and to promote the economic autonomy of women, were convinced that domestic space must be altered in such a way as to make these reforms possible.[14]

Catherine Beecher was a reformer who accepted a conventional definition of the domestic world as women's sphere, but she argued

that women should rule the home in their capacity as skilled pro-
fessionals, and she designed a number of houses during the second
half of the nineteenth century which made the kitchen area the
central focus of the house.

Melusina Fay Pierce was one of the first women in the United
States to make a detailed critique of domestic labour. She demanded
pay for housework, she organized the women of her town to get it
and she was a great proponent of what she called co-operative
housekeeping. Co-operative housekeeping would consist of groups
of fifteen to twenty-three women who would organize co-operative
associations to perform all their domestic work collectively and
then charge their husbands for these services. The association
would have a headquarters equipped with the appropriate mech-
anical devices for cooking, laundry and so on. It would employ
former servants who were skilled in particular tasks, and these
women would be paid wages equivalent to those of skilled male
workers. The association would charge retail prices for cooked
food, laundry, clothing and provisions – cash on delivery! Pierce
believed that when co-operating women had established their domestic industries in a central building, women architects should de-
sign houses without kitchens.

In her book *Women and Economics* Charlotte Perkins Gilman described a world where women worked for wages outside the home,
where they had economic independence and where they lived with
their families in private kitchenless houses or in apartments connected to central kitchens, dining rooms and day centres. Gilman
believed that new domestic environments would promote the evol-
ution of socialism, a view which has also been held to varying
degrees by socialist governments in our own time.

Nineteenth-century science fiction novels, like those of the twen-
tieth century, also linked the refiguration of social and sexual relations to changes in spatial relations and domestic environments
(Moore, 1990b). Novelists and reformers alike recognized the way
in which the organization of the material world encodes dominant
cultural meanings and discourses. The social practices and activities
carried out in symbolically constructed space act as a mnemonic for
dominant sets of conceptual and social relations. One example of
this is that if a Carmelite nun spends sixty years in a Carmelite
convent – all her life, in other words – she will kneel in the same
place, at the same time, 42,800 times (D. Williams, 1975). This re-

veals the crucial point about the relationship between gender and material culture. It is not that the material world, as a form of cultural discourse, reflects the natural division of the world into women and men, but rather that cultural discourses, including the organization of the material world, actually produce gender difference in and through their workings. It is not that our bodies naturally evince gender differences, or any other form of difference, it is rather that these differences are produced as an effect upon them. Teresa de Lauretis describes the process rather well in another context:

> Most of us – those of us who are women; to those who are men this will not apply – probably check the F box rather than the M box when filling out an application form. It would hardly occur to us to mark M. It would be like cheating, or, worse, not existing, like erasing ourselves from the world . . . For since the very first time we put a check mark on the little square next to the F on the form, we have officially entered the sex-gender system, the social relations of gender, and have become engendered as women; that is to say, not only do other people consider us females, but from that moment on *we* have been representing ourselves as women. Now I ask, isn't that the same as saying that . . . while we thought that we were marking the F on the form, in fact the F was marking itself on us? (1987: 11–12)

The moral of the story is, be careful how you tick the box.

5

SOCIAL IDENTITIES AND THE POLITICS OF REPRODUCTION

The analysis of the household and the conceptual and empirical difficulties inherent in defining the relationship between the family and the household are areas of concern in all the social sciences. In the last fifteen years there have been two major developments in this field. The first has been a shift from the analysis of the household as a bounded unit towards a view which stresses its permeability. Current critiques of the household point to the enormous variability in household forms, structures and activities both within and between societies. They also stress that households are not bounded units and that their internal structures and workings both produce and are produced by larger-scale cultural, economic and political processes. The permeability of the household unit and the observable variability of its forms have led to considerable anxiety about its analytical and methodological utility. In relation to the analysis of the household it has been suggested that the appropriate question should not be 'Where is the household?' but 'What are the significant units of production, consumption and investment in this region/group/people; and what are the major flows and transfers of resources between individuals and units?' (Guyer and Peters, 1987: 208).

The second major development in the study of the household has been a move away from the folk ideology of the household as a 'haven from a heartless world', where relations between family members are characterized by sharing, and are seen as essentially equal and co-operative. This move signals a *rapprochement* between feminist analyses of family/household structures and mainstream disciplinary models in anthropology and, to a lesser extent, in economics. It is clear that the feminist understanding of the family/ household over the last fifteen years has been diametrically opposed to the anthropological models of the household influenced by Chayanovian economics and Marxist theory (for example, Sahlins, 1974), and to the somewhat similar views of the household manifest in the 'new home economics' (Becker, 1976, 1981).[1] This is predominantly because such models emphasize sharing and altruism, whereas feminist scholars have characterized the family/ household as the site of women's oppression and as the locus of conflicts of interest between women and men (among them Harris, 1981; Mackintosh, 1979; Barrett, 1980; A. Whitehead, 1981; Hartmann, 1981). One result of this *rapprochement* between feminist theorizing and mainstream anthropology and economics has been the emergence of a view of the household which sees it as a locus of competing interests, rights, obligations and resources, where household members are often involved in bargaining, negotiation and possibly even conflict.

A number of alternative models for the analysis of the household based on contracts, bargaining and negotiation have now been proposed by economists and other social scientists (for example, Folbre, 1984, 1988; Fapohunda, 1978, 1988; Jones, 1983, 1986). In such models questions of power and ideology, formerly ignored by structural-functionalist and economistic approaches to the household, become prominent (Hart, 1993). This new focus on power and ideology is a response to the recognition that the outcome of bargaining and negotiation between household members is never simply determined by economic factors, such as access to resources.[2] Socially and historically specific views about the rights, responsibilities and needs of particular individuals are at least as important, and often more important, in determining the outcome of bargaining and negotiation. As Nancy Folbre has argued, the bargaining power of individuals cannot be defined purely with reference to individual assets, because bargaining power is 'significantly affected by the cultural and political implications of membership in certain demographic groups' (1988: 256–7).

The problem, then, for the contemporary analysis of the household is to examine precisely how bargaining power in the household is significantly affected by questions of power and ideology. But since we know that the household is a permeable rather than a bounded unit, we can assume that the processes involved are two-way ones – in other words, that the workings of households have something to do with the functioning of social, economic and political processes outside them. On the whole, it is fair to say that social scientists have been rather more successful in developing theories which account for how larger-scale processes determine, or perhaps simply constrain, the workings of smaller social units – like villages or lineages or households or persons – than they have in proposing theories which explain how smaller social units influence larger-scale social, economic and political processes. Most practising social scientists would probably claim that they are concerned with both sets of relations, and that they spend a great deal of time turning themselves on their heads to look at the problem from both ends simultaneously. This topsy-turvy struggle is an admirable one, and it underlines the point that there are many things in social science which are extremely easy to hint at but very difficult to analyse in practice.

One way in which this problem of multiple or dialectical determination has been approached before in anthropology and sociology is through the animated debate that took place between the Marxists and the feminists in the 1970s and 1980s. This debate was ostensibly about the relationship between production and reproduction, and, of necessity, it was concerned with the relationship between the family and/or household and larger-scale economic and political processes. However, underlying the arguments put forward was the assumption that women have a different relation to the mode of production than do men. The ultimate focus of the argument was thus on production, even though it was supposed to be about the relationship between production and reproduction. The net result was a familiar overvaluing and overestimation of production in relation to reproduction. I want to argue in this essay that we cannot hope to comprehend the workings of households or the links which bind them to larger-scale institutions and processes unless we take into account what have been termed the relations of reproduction, and cease to think of these relations as being necessarily secondary to relations of production. A similar argument has recently been made by the anthropologist Sandy Robertson in his book *Beyond the Family* (1991). But Robertson's work is flawed by his tendency to conflate various kinds of reproduction which should be kept analytically separate.

In the 1970s and 1980s Olivia Harris and others argued that reproduction is of a three-fold kind: social reproduction, the reproduction of the labour force and human or biological reproduction (Harris, 1981; Harris and Young, 1981). This feminist deconstruction of reproduction was both necessary and helpful, but it failed – at least as far as the debate in anthropology was concerned – to do two very important things. First, it neglected to point out that reproduction is not something which is confined to the household or the family, and that a consideration of relations of reproduction is crucial to an understanding of political and economic institutions beyond the household. Secondly, it did not succeed in developing an adequate analysis of social reproduction. In both feminist and Marxist writing in anthropology there has been a tendency to treat social reproduction as though it is simply synonymous with the reproduction of the household. Thereafter, it is straightforwardly assumed that the reproduction of society follows quite naturally from the reproduction of its most basic units – that is, households.[3]

Sandy Robertson avoids the first failing, and he advances our understanding of the relationship between households and larger-scale economic processes by insisting that 'there are some aspects of the elaborate political and economic institutions of . . . societies which can only be explained by understanding the influence of reproductive processes' (1991: 52). But he does not avoid the second pitfall precisely because he conflates social reproduction both with biological reproduction and with the reproduction of the labour force. The main premise of his book is that economic institutions, including banking firms and the modern state, have to be analysed from the point of view of their role in the work of reproduction because their chief function in social life is to combat the instability of the reproductive cycle. Where once we might have invested in our kin, we now invest in banks. As Robertson says:

> Money, markets and banks have made many aspects of reproductive organisation more efficient – for some, if not for all. Along with the web of political institutions of which they are a part, they provide means for combating the insecurities of the reproductive cycle. (1991: 91)

The reproduction of society is assumed once again to follow unproblematically from the reproduction of individuals and households. Banks may be involved in the reproduction of society through the mechanisms by which they combat the insecurities of the reproductive cycle – by providing mechanisms for saving and investment, for example – but ultimately they will be dependent on individual households for the production and supply of persons, and by this Robertson means, of course, biological individuals.

On one level there is nothing problematic about what Robertson has to say, because societies will always be dependent on the reproduction of biological individuals for their continuity. However, there is obviously much more to social reproduction than merely the production of babies. The problem for societies, after all, is not just to produce sufficient babies – though there are many societies which experience just this problem; the main difficulty is rather to produce and reproduce persons with particular social identities, that is, persons who are appropriately differentiated socially. I would argue that the key to understanding the two-way relationship between households and larger-scale economic and political processes and institutions is the question of social identities. When societies produce individuals, they do not just produce biological individuals, they produce social and socialized persons. This process is certainly never complete or straightforward, and it will always involve both conflict and contradiction. There is no such thing as the perfectly socialized person (see chapters 2, 3 and 4) appropriately adapted to the functional needs of society. Such an individual does not exist, because the social divisions on which social relations and social identities depend produce differences both between social groups and within individual subjects. However, the social identities considered in this essay are those of a categorical nature, and the issue at hand is one about the way in which these categorical identities are constitutive of economic and political processes. In order to examine why the production and reproduction of social identities is the key to understanding social reproduction, it is necessary to return briefly to the level of the household.

Social identities

Folbre's insight that the outcome of bargaining and negotiation within the household cannot be determined purely by reference to economic assets because it is always significantly affected by the cultural and political implications of membership in certain demographic groups refers directly to the importance of socially established differences between people. Such socially established differences draw on normative understandings and practices which are linked to accepted power differences and ideologies. A recognition of the importance of the normative understandings and practices associated with gender ideologies has led some scholars to develop the notion of contractual relations between household members (Jones, 1983, 1986; A. Whitehead, 1981, 1984). In an early article Ann Whitehead introduced the idea of a conjugal contract to describe 'the terms on which products and income, produced by the labour of both husband and wife, are divided to meet their personal and collective needs' (1981: 108). This underscores the point that when people discuss the terms of the marital contract or the allocation of resources within the household, they usually do so in terms of rights and needs. Rights and needs are intimately related. Women, for example, may have rights to pooled resources within the household, but their ability to exercise those rights is likely to be determined by various cultural and contextual evaluations of need.

Whitehead suggests that the terms and nature of marital contracts – she is talking here not about legal contracts, but about normative understandings of the marital relation – change according to the location of the household in the wider economy. She argues that certain gender ideologies, such as the construction of motherhood, mean that individuals are constrained as to the kinds of strategies they can employ in the processes of bargaining and renegotiation, and that this becomes particularly crucial at moments of rapid social and economic change. She makes the very important point that inequalities of power are made manifest in the interpretation of the terms of the contract, and that these give rise to material conflicts of interest between women and men. The ability to provide an interpretation of the terms of the marital contract, or indeed of any set of normative practices and understandings, is, of course, a political ability. Definitions of terms, and interpretations of normative practices and understandings, are political definitions. They are political because they can, in principle, be redefined and contested, and because they will always have material consequences. Bargaining and negotiation between women and men, and indeed between persons of the same gender, are often about definitions and interpretations, and it is for this reason that gender relations are always involved with power. Power is an aspect of gender relations.

Conjugal arrangements, residence rights, inheritance laws – all of which are relevant to household analysis – not only describe sets of social and economic relations, but also encode ideas about gender ideologies, and about the different natures, tasks and roles of women and men in society. A lack of comprehension about and analytical attention to gender ideologies is a feature of many anthropological and economic approaches to the household, especially those concerned with policy implementation. It is often implied in such research that gender ideologies are just ideas, cultural beliefs and notions which are somehow attached to economic and political processes, but are not constitutive of them. This kind of argument ignores the extent to which economic processes, such as the differentiation of tasks by gender, negotiations between husbands and wives over income distribution and discussions with daughters and sons about educational provision and residence requirements, are actually a set of practical activities which operationalize gender ideologies. They are, therefore, in some sense the outcome of local ideas about the appropriate behaviour of women and men. Gender ideologies and other forms of difference, such as race and class, which draw on social identities are crucial to understanding social reproduction, both at the level of the household and at the level of the state. This point can be most clearly made by examining how social identities that are based on ideologies or 'naturalized' cultural conventions are implicated in power structures and in the structuring of inequalities.

Differentiated social identities are related to the exercise of power, because the very definitions of those identities are connected to normative or conventional explanations for the social order, as well as to legitimations of that order. This is most particularly the case where social definitions of identity are based on ascriptive characteristics which themselves form the basis for power relations and institutionalized inequalities. In such cases – for example, landowner/peasant, white person/black person, husband/wife, father/son – social definitions of identity serve to naturalize inequality. The power to name, to define a social identity and to ascribe characteristics to that identity is a political power (Margolis, 1989: 339; Bourdieu, 1977, 1990b). It is on the basis of the naturalized differences between these identities that the rights and needs of particular individuals are established. Rights and needs are differentially distributed between different sorts of persons, and the ability to define a social identity is the ability to assign appropriate rights and needs. Gender, race and class differences, for example, encode ideas about the rights and needs of the persons so differentiated. Furthermore, this process of differentiation privileges or disadvantages such persons in their capacity to make claims on resources, both material and symbolic, in the domestic arena and beyond.

In considering these issues in relation to the analysis of social reproduction what is important is the recognition that the production of people is not just a matter of reproducing biological individuals, or even of reproducing the labour force; it is a matter of producing particular sorts of persons with specific attributes in ways that are congruent with socially established patterns of power. Thus, what makes households distinctive is not that they produce people and thereby reproduce society, but that they – along with many other institutions – produce specific sorts of persons with specific social identities, and particular rights and needs.

Rights and needs

In order to understand the relationship between rights and needs, and to examine the way in which rights and needs are operationalized in social relations and interactions, it is necessary to focus attention on discourses about rights and needs, and to look at the way in which issues about rights and needs are framed. Nancy Fraser has suggested a very powerful way of analysing such discourses. Fraser begins with the idea that needs claims always have a contextual and contested character (1989: 163). She argues that most theories of the politics of need assume that the only issue is whether or not various predefined needs will be met. Such an assumption deflects attention from the fact that it is not just the satisfaction of needs, but need interpretations which are politically contested. People's needs are not simply given and unproblematic, they always require an interpretation. Furthermore, Fraser argues that most theories of the politics of need assume that it does not matter who interprets the needs in question, or from what perspective or in the light of what interests. Fraser suggests an alternative approach to the politics of needs that depends on identifying three 'moments' that are analytically distinct, but interrelated in practice:

1   'the struggle to establish or deny the political status of a given need'; that is, the attempt to define the need as a matter of legitimate political concern or to categorize it as a non-political matter;
2   disputation over the interpretation of the need; that is, the process of argumentation that determines who has the power to define the need and thereby to establish what would satisfy it;
3   contestation over the satisfaction of the need; that is, the fight to secure or withhold provision (1989: 164).

Following Nancy Fraser, it is possible to suggest a way of analysing how the struggle over needs interpretations links the household to wider social networks and institutions, including the state. This is most evident in contemporary societies because of state involvement in social reproduction. Fraser's method for analysing the politics of need can be illustrated by reference to the mechanisms through which the government of the United Kingdom has consistently tried to divest itself of the costs of social reproduction in the last ten years or so. For example, Fraser's first moment or stage, the struggle to define a need as a legitimate political concern or to categorize it as a non-political matter, can be seen clearly at work in the question of the provision of child care for working mothers. The debate in the UK has been about whether or not the government will provide nursery places for pre-school children. Hardest hit by the government's failure to make such provision are single parents, most of whom are women. The prohibitive cost of child care often means that they simply cannot afford to work, and the result is that they have to struggle to support their families on whatever welfare provision is available. This policy affects the poorer sections of the population most directly, and contributes to their ongoing impoverishment. In the inner-city areas many of the poorer people affected by this policy are black, and thus the struggle over child-care provision reinforces differences of race and class simultaneously.

What is interesting about this debate is the way in which the government has sought to justify its policy by representing children as a personal and private responsibility. If you choose to have children, then you must look after them; you cannot expect the state to do so. This statement is a very powerful one precisely because it appears so obvious, so natural. If you want the state to look after your children, then there is something wrong with you as a parent, and, by extension, if you want to go out to work instead of looking after your children, then there is something wrong with you as a mother. The government position on single-parent families is that they find themselves in difficulties only because they are improper, incomplete families. The result is that proper families, proper parents and proper mothers do not have these problems, and thus child care is not a state responsibility, and there can be no way in which a legitimate political claim can be made on the state for its provision.

An example of Fraser's second moment or stage, the struggle over the interpretation of a need and therefore the determination of what could be deemed to satisfy that need, can be provided by looking at what has happened to the care for the mentally ill in British society. In England and Wales in the mid-1950s 150,000 people were in mental hospitals; now there are only 60,000. The government proposes that this number should decrease further, and plans to close thirty-two of the remaining ninety big psychiatric hospitals over the next five years. During the 1980s the government constantly argued that most mentally ill people should be returned to care in the community. This argument – which makes good economic sense since the cost of keeping a person in a hospital is £72 a day compared with 29p per day for caring for them in the community – draws on views propounded both by the left and by liberal lobbying bodies which criticize the incarceration, institutionalization and stigmatization associated with long-stay mental hospitals. People who suffer from treatable conditions and are able to lead normal and autonomous lives should not be shut up in institutions for life.

This humane view was co-opted by the Thatcher government in ways which made subsequent government policy very difficult to criticize, even though the government's economic motives were plain to all. However, what is of interest here is the way in which the needs of the mentally ill were redefined over the 1980s, and in that process there was a redefinition of what could be deemed to satisfy those needs. Care in the community rather than incarceration suddenly became appropriate, not because it had never been suggested before, but because there had been a shift in the power struggle over the definition of the needs of the mentally ill. In the process of this redefinition of need the social identity of the mentally ill was transformed also because what it meant to be mentally ill altered. The importance of this alteration is evident when we consider that changes in the definition of need and in the definition of the social identity involved gave rise to changes in the nature of resource flows.

Fraser's third stage or moment in the analysis of the politics of need – the fight to secure or withhold provision – can be illustrated with reference to government policy on housing in the UK, where homelessness has increased steadily in the last fifteen years. Exact figures are hard to come by, but estimates give the number of people living homeless on the streets of London as 4,000, though after the £96 million scheme initiated by the government in 1992, it is thought that this figure may have dropped to around 2,500. Housing in the UK is an interesting case because it is a recognized need, but not necessarily one the government feels it has to meet. While housing can be considered a need, it is not necessarily a right, and thus considerable debate ensues as to whether or not provision should be made. In the past local government did make provision, but over the last fifteen years they have been increasingly prevented from doing so by the national government, which has insisted that local councils sell off their housing stock.

The three examples I have just given emphasize the importance of the role of the state in social reproduction. There are many other institutions, such as the education system, the job market and the armed forces, which are involved in social reproduction, but the main point is that social reproduction is not something which goes on solely within household, nor is the reproduction of society something which comes about merely through the reproduction of households. A further point which becomes evident in Fraser's analysis of the politics of needs is the way in which any argument about needs necessarily involves a discussion about rights, and together debates about rights and needs invoke social identities, as well as the meanings invested in those categorical identities. The result is that much of what goes on in the politics of needs interpretation has to do with discourses on social identity and with attempts to define the nature of certain identities.

Fraser attempts to approach this problem through the analysis of the historically and culturally specific ensemble of discourses available to members of a social collectivity when making claims against one another (1989: 164–5). Amongst these resources, she includes:

1   the recognized idioms in which one can press claims, for example, needs talk, rights talk, interests talk. Needs, rights and interests become politicized when black people, women or workers, for example, start to contest previously subordinated identities and roles, and thereby to oppose the conventional and frequently disadvantageous needs interpretations embodied in and assigned to those identities (Fraser, 1989: 171). In such situations new needs emerge and become legitimate political issues, and new interpretations of old needs are offered. Both these processes give rise to the redefinition of social identities; new social groupings and categories of person emerge; old categories and groupings are redefined.

2   Fraser discusses the vocabularies available for pressing claims within recognized idioms, such as needs talk, rights talk and so on. These vocabularies can be of many different kinds and include administrative vocabularies, religious vocabularies, feminist vocabularies and modernizing vocabularies. In the UK changes in public appreciation of the rights and needs of women – changes which are clearly linked to women's increasing political and economic importance as voters and workers – have led to the emergence of new vocabularies both for the description of these new needs and rights and for the purposes of political persuasion. One clear case is provided by the development of two new terms: marital rape and date rape. Until recently most British people would probably have thought that both were a contradiction in terms. Marital rape was declared illegal only in 1991 in England and Wales, and date rape came on to the popular agenda as a result of the William Kennedy Smith and Mike Tyson rape trials in the United States. Date rape gained particular salience in the public imagination after the publication in February 1992 of a survey conducted in England at Cambridge University, where one in nine female students reported experiencing rape by a friend, acquaintance, fellow student or work colleague.

3   Fraser notes the paradigms or forms of argumentation accepted as authoritative in adjudicating between conflicting claims. She is concerned here with such things as whether conflicts are resolved by appeal to conventional understandings, to routinized ways of doing things, to elders or to religious leaders, or

whether conflicts are resolved by voting or by privileging the interpretations of those whose needs are in question. She recognizes, of
course, that conflicts are frequently resolved – if they are resolved –
through a mixture of such methods. Power and ideology are most
explicitly at work in determining what patterns of argumentation
will be accepted as authoritative. This is often evident within households, where husbands have both the power and the right to determine what is right for others. In such situations an hierarchization
of needs and rights inevitably emerges, and this hierarchization is
congruent with patterns of dominance and power. What is interesting, however, is that patterns of authorization can be challenged, as,
for example, in the case of marital rape, where the law now challenges older, conventional understandings of the rights and responsibilities of men and women in marriage. Conflict thus emerges not
only between needs claims and interpretations, but also between
the different groups or interests who wish to insist that only they
have the right and the power to arbitrate between conflicting claims.
One very powerful example here is provided by the case of abortion. Abortion, under very specific circumstances, is legal in the UK,
but since its legalization in the 1960s several attempts have been
made to overturn parliament's decision. Intense lobbying on all
sides has involved statements and counter-statements, such as 'this
is a moral issue', 'this is an issue of conscience', 'this is an issue of
women's rights', 'this is an issue of foetal rights'. Such statements
are designed to frame the question of abortion as something which
should properly be the domain of the private individual or the
family or the Church or the State. Different interest groups may
acknowledge the right of others to speak on the matter, but they
want in the end to assert that they should have the final say, that
they should be the final arbiters.

   4   Fraser identifies the importance of modes of subjectification;
that is, the ways in which various discourses position people as
specific sorts of subjects endowed with specific sorts of capacities
(1989: 165). The interpretation of rights and needs is always bound
up with the constitution of social identities. However, Fraser is
drawing attention here to the way in which specific claims construct
individuals or groups as particular kinds of people with particular
characteristics. For example, it must be apparent that if the UK
government is going to return mentally ill people to care in the

community, there must be carers in the community. These carers, who are most often explicitly identified in the practical implementation of this policy, are women. No one in their right mind would suggest that a forty-year-old man should stay at home to look after a sick parent. The assumption that women are carers is based on a further series of assumptions both about the nature and capacities of women and about mothers. Women are at home in the community to care because they are mothers and do not work, or if they do work it is secondary to their maternal/caring role and they will therefore be happy to give it up.

A related set of assumptions sustains segregation in the labour market. No matter how many women work all their adult lives, the prevailing view is still that work is something temporary for women because they will give it up when they have children. Women in the UK who want to continue working after the birth of their first child often find themselves under tremendous pressure to leave their jobs. Living with the label 'bad mother' is a truly burdensome occupation. Women continually find themselves defined by the label 'mother', and it is this label which then defines their relation to work, to social relations, to sexuality and even to life. There is nothing natural about motherhood or womanhood. Every woman knows that the meaning and experience of motherhood and womanhood for the white middle classes has little to do with their meaning and experience for black working-class women, for example. Other social categories are similarly socially constructed, and they are at their most powerful when they appear most natural, most transparent, most taken for granted.

This analysis of some of the resources which people draw on to press claims emphasizes that in any given context there are a very diverse number of discourses which can be employed, and that whilst certain discourses may be predominantly employed at one level or in one particular context, they affect claim procedures at other levels and in other contexts. For example, state legislation regarding mother and child health and welfare may not displace local understandings of the rights and responsibilities of motherhood, but the views of motherhood encoded in such legislation will affect negotiations between husbands and wives within the household regarding such things as women's paid employment and health care for children. Similarly, local understandings about the appropriate behaviour of women and men, and of the sexual division of labour, will affect women's participation in employment, in development programmes and in education, and will thus become utilized as a resource in the discourses of experts, academics and administrators.

In many cases competing discourses about rights and needs implicitly and explicitly evoke and invoke each other. Discussion about the responsibilities of motherhood which involve women in caring and providing for children can, in some circumstances, refer implicitly to the responsibilities of fatherhood and the necessity to provide properly for the family. Thus, men who would seek to retain a large portion of their income for personal needs cannot press the claim that their wives should take responsibility for feeding the children and for providing other household needs without evoking the alternative interpretation.

However, it is not just that there are competing discourses about rights and needs, but also that such discourses are stratified. They are stratified because societies are stratified, differentiated into social groups with unequal status, power and access to resources, cross-cut by major axes of inequality, such as race, gender, age, class, ethnicity and religion. According to Fraser, this means that competing discourses about rights and needs are also stratified and organized 'in ways which are congruent with societal patterns of dominance and subordination' (1989: 165). It follows from this that some discourses are hegemonic, authorized and sanctioned, whilst others are non-hegemonic, disqualified and discounted (Fraser, 1989: 165). This leads Fraser to the crucial point that interpretations of needs (and rights) are not just interpretations, but also practical acts and interventions:

> From this perspective, needs talk appears as a site of struggle where groups with unequal discursive (and nondiscursive) resources compete to establish as hegemonic their respective interpretations of legitimate social needs. Dominant groups articulate need interpretations intended to exclude, defuse, and/or co-opt counter interpretations. Subordinate or oppositional groups, on the other hand, articulate need interpretations intended to challenge, displace and/ or modify dominant ones. In neither case are the interpretations simply 'representations'. In both cases, rather, they are acts and interventions. (1989: 166)

The system of redistribution

In the preceding sections I have been concerned to show how bargaining and negotiation cannot be seen as a straightforward outcome of economic assets and that what is needed is a clear understanding of how social identities – in particular, those based on gender – are implicated in the determination of discourses about the rights and needs of specific sorts of individuals. In this section I develop the concept of the system of redistribution.[4] This concept takes gender relations as constitutive of economic processes and thus offers a means of integrating the analysis of power and ideology with patterns of production, consumption, distribution and investment. It also permits an analysis of the links between different levels of social life (household, lineage, region, state) in a way that demonstrates that those linkages are themselves gendered. The underlying premise of the notion of a system of redistribution is that it is the mechanisms of redistribution in society, rather than the processes of production and reproduction, which are crucial to understanding the relationship between households and larger-scale economic and social processes and institutions. A further assumption is that social identities are integral to the system of redistribution and that they structure the nature and direction of resource flows within the household and beyond. Thus, when we come to consider the theoretical utility of the production/reproduction debate, we can see that these notions only offer us theoretical purchase in so far as they adequately treat the question of the production and reproduction of social identities.

The sexual division of labour, whereby different productive and reproductive tasks are assigned to women and men, always creates the necessity for redistribution both within the domestic domain and within the social collectivity as a whole. It matters not whether we are considering a capitalist system, where the production of material needs takes place outside the household, or a non-capitalist or peripherally capitalist system, where household members are engaged in production for own-consumption and for the market. Under any sexual division of labour, where reproductive tasks fall disproportionately to persons of either gender – in the vast majority of cases these persons will be women – the system of redistribution will be gendered, just as the system of production is gendered.

Gender ideologies and differentiated social identities of all kinds –
especially those based on race and class – are implicated in this
gendering process. They bestow the rights and entitlements that
provide the framework within which bargaining and negotiation
about redistribution take place. The concept of a system of redistribution shifts the focus of interest in social science analysis away
from a primary concern with production and the relations of production. An emphasis on production obscures the fact that gender
relations and the differences of race and class are structured
through redistribution as well as through relations of production
and reproduction.

Gender and rice

In order to demonstrate the fruitfulness of an approach based on the
concept of a system of redistribution, it is necessary to examine a
concrete example. One of the most sensitive and interesting of
recent studies is Judith Carney's and Michael Watts's analysis of
Mandinka rice growers in the Gambia, West Africa (1990). This
study is particularly apt because it takes gender relations as central
to the analysis of economic processes, and it sees struggles over
work as a struggle over meaning and over the redefinition of rights
and responsibilities.

There is a marked sexual division of labour in Mandinka society.
Women are responsible for child care, cooking and domestic work,
and provide the labour involved in threshing and winnowing.
Thus, the burden of reproductive labour falls disproportionately on
women. A sexual division of labour is also evident in crop production; women customarily grow rice, while men engage in the
upland production of groundnuts, millet and sorghum. Mandinka
households distinguish between two types of land use on family
held land: household production on collective fields known as
maruo; and individual production on plots known as *kamanyango*.
Under conventional arrangements, women have an obligation to
provide labour on the collective fields as part of the marital contract,
and individual household members gain usufruct rights on
kamanyango plots in return for their labour on the household field
(Carney and Watts, 1990: 219–20).

The introduction of small-scale pump irrigated rice projects in the 1960s and 1970s saw the emergence of conflict and tension between women and men, as the latter gained control over the irrigation schemes by clearing land and thus establishing individual ownership, and/or by designating the plots as household fields and then drawing on female labour obligations to cultivate them. Male control over pump irrigated rice – a crop they had formerly not specialized in – was fostered by the development agencies who 'channelled the Green Revolution inputs to household heads on the assumption that Mandinka family farms operated as a joint utility function' (Carney and Watts, 1990: 221). In this situation, where property control and the classification of plot type are crucial because they permit household heads to activate claims to female labour, it is quite clear that a change in the nature of rice cultivation involved women and men in bargaining and negotiation not only over the rights they have in household property, but over the rights they have in each other.

The system of redistribution in Mandinka society comes about as the result of the divisions of labour established in the productive and reproductive domains – without divisions of labour, systems of redistribution are not, of course, necessary. In all cases processes of redistribution are subject to bargaining, negotiation and re-evaluation in the light of local concepts of the rights and needs of different categories of individuals. However, it follows from this that, through processes of bargaining and negotiation, rights and needs are themselves open to change and renegotiation. This is the situation which confronted Mandinka women and men. But there is a further point. Local discourses about rights and needs are inevitably linked to similar discourses which originate at other social levels or in other institutions, such as development agencies or the State. These discourses not only shape resource flows within the larger system of redistribution, but they may be used also as strategic resources themselves in the bargaining and negotiation that goes on between women and men within the household and at the local level. Mandinka women and men were very aware, for example, that development agencies were channelling inputs to household heads on the assumption that the Mandinka household operated as a joint utility function. The men responded positively because it enhanced their control over rice production; the women resisted the process of redefinition and the increased demands on their labour which that redefinition brought about (Carney and Watts, 1990: 222–5).

Praxis and social identity

Throughout their article Carney and Watts constantly emphasize that in reproducing a particular set of social relations people also reproduce an experience of those relations. The struggle over access to economic resources is simultaneously a struggle over definitions and meanings. For example, the definition of land types has consequences for labour control, and changes in the nature of labour allocation and control give new meaning, both practically and discursively, to what it means to be a wife, a husband and a dependant. Thus, social identities are fully engaged in the processes of bargaining and negotiation that shape access to economic resources, as well as the direction of resource flows both within the household and beyond. Such resource flows are the outcome of the system of redistribution, and it is through processes of redistribution that social identities are themselves reproduced. It is for this reason that the concept of a system of redistribution contains no necessary connotation of reciprocal exchange or equalization. The full engagement of social identities in the bargaining and negotiations that shape the system of redistribution means that resource flows within the system are partial outcomes of conventional understandings of the rights and needs of particular sorts of individuals. These conventional understandings can be seen as local theories of entitlement, and such theories are always bound up with ideologies and with unequal power relations.

It is the relationship between ideologies, power and entitlements established in the context of the bargaining and negotiation that takes place over resource flows which emphasizes the point that although patterns of contestation exist, and although the routinization of convention means that regularities occur, the final outcome of any struggle cannot be predetermined. This is because local theories of entitlement and local ideologies of gender, race and class are themselves potentially subject to change through the processes of bargaining and negotiation. Local understandings and conventions are therefore best understood as actual resources which are drawn on in the process of bargaining and negotiation, rather than as norms which determine the outcome of such processes. It is through the negotiations that shape the outcome of the system of redistribution that social identities are themselves reproduced and opened up to potential change. Thus, to say that the system of redistribution is the product of the relationship between production and reproduction in a given context is to emphasize once again that reproduction not only involves biological reproduction and the reproduction of the labour force, but also includes social reproduction, a critical part of which is the reproduction of particular sorts of persons endowed with specific social identities.

Engagement in the system of redistribution provides individual persons with an experience of the meaning of gender, and with the meaning of other forms of differentiated identity – meaning is only given to difference through practical engagement. However, the very fact of practical engagement in the system of redistribution ties the experience of social identities, and of their construction, both to processes and relations within the domain of the household and to wider economic and political networks.

If, as I have suggested, the system of redistribution is a consequence of the particular relationship established between production and reproduction in a given context, then it would be legitimate to enquire how this concept could be usefully applied in instances where a relationship between productive and reproductive labour is not immediately apparent within the household. Two clear examples might be female-headed households and single-person households. The first point to be made here is that the system of redistribution shapes resource flows within the household and beyond, and links the household to wider economic relations and networks. Thus, both female-headed and single-person households are inserted into a wider system of redistribution which operates at the local, regional, national and international level.

A second point concerns the way in which community and supra-community understandings of differentiated social identities, and of the rights and needs on which those identities are based, are constitutive of the system of redistribution. This means, for example, that female household heads are engaged in sets of social and productive relations with others in their community in order to secure access to such things as land, labour, welfare provision, education for their children and alimony, depending on the economic and political context in which they find themselves. Thus, these households are situated in a system of redistribution which is materially and discursively structured according to local and supra-local understandings of the rights and needs of particular sorts of persons. For example, the local community may have views about widows as opposed to women who have been left behind by a migrant labourer husband, and these views in conjunction with each woman's particular circumstances – such as level of economic resources, education, number of children, personality type and strength of kin network – will provide the context in which bargaining and negotiation within the local system of redistribution will take place. The outcome of particular negotiations may also be materially affected by supra-local discourses about the rights and needs of particular kinds of persons, which might be made manifest through the targeted provision of advice and/or credit provided by extension services or local development projects, or through such things as state legislation on school attendance and the provision of pensions.

This situation applies equally to single-person households in industrial economies, where supra-local discourses on the rights and needs of particular sorts of persons take shape in such things as housing and welfare policy, tax assessment and pension arrangements. These discourses shape the wider system of redistribution within which the household is embedded. In developed capitalist economies much of the domestic labour necessary for the reproduction of single-person households is provided through the service sector of the economy. This sector, like all others, is itself structured according to the system of redistribution and according to the differentiated social identities on which the system itself is based.

The actual relations of redistribution vary from one context to another, and are crucially dependent on the extent of market integration, the degree of segmentation of the labour market and the level of the development of the service sector of the economy. However, what does not vary is the necessity for a system of redistribution. Redistribution is an ongoing process and it is necessary precisely because different people are constructed as having different rights and needs.

6

MASTER NARRATIVES:
ANTHROPOLOGY AND WRITING

Post-modernism has arrived in anthropology, as is evidenced by recent concern with forms of anthropological writing and with the nature and politics of representation. This 'new ethnography', as the post-modernist critique within the discipline is known, turns on two interrelated issues: what is it that anthropologists represent or claim to represent in their texts; and by what authority do anthropologists make these representations?[1] The answers to these questions necessarily involve a number of considerations. Underlying the 'new ethnography' are anxieties about anthropology's role in the construction and maintenance of western imperialism and neo-imperialism. A number of authors have expressed the hope that through new types of experimental ethnographic writing anthropology can expose the global systems of power relations which are embedded in traditional representations of the 'other' and 'other cultures.' Post-modernist anthropologists call attention to the constructed nature of cultural accounts, and they seek to develop new forms of writing, such as those predicated on dialogue, intertextuality and heteroglossia to unmask and displace the unitary authority of the anthropologist as author. Anthropology as a discipline can no longer be held to speak with automatic authority for 'others' previously defined as unable to speak for themselves, being 'primitive', 'pre-literate,' 'without history' (Clifford, 1986: 10). The idea that what anthropologists represent in their texts is an 'other' culture is seriously in doubt. Since all cultural and historical accounts are partial, constructed ones, there can be no question of providing a single authoritative account of another culture. Culture is a domain of contested and negotiated meanings. Anthropologists do not represent other cultures, they invent them, construct them, and they do so through the process of writing or, more properly, through the process of textualization (Wagner, 1975; Clifford, 1986: ch. 1; Minh-ha, 1989, 1991), since we would want to include here not only conventional written ethnographies but also ethnographic films, photographs and representations of all kinds.

It is quite clear that this process of textualization is much more than merely a process of knowledge production; it is a process of knowledge creation. This point has been made very engagingly with regard to early writings on southern and eastern Africa.[2]

> When we think of the so-called nineteenth century discovery of Africa, we usually think of the professional explorer and soldier, the handful of men whom Conrad called 'militant geographers'. Yet, ordinary literate people also discovered Africa, through their churches, mission societies and a number of written genres that were offered primarily as entertainment. (Thornton, 1983: 503)

For, aside from the popular and expensively produced travellers' tales, there were also other texts which reached a much wider audience in Britain and Europe. Some of the most accomplished writers and ethnographers of Africa in the nineteenth century were missionaries – David Livingstone, Robert Moffat, John Roscoe. These men wrote for audiences which were essentially made up of church-goers, the ordinary women and men of the congregation. They wrote church bulletins, missionary tracts and letters to the press, and when they were 'home', they spoke to large audiences in crowded church halls all over Britain (Thornton, 1983: 504). As a result the discovery of Africa (so called) was actually a discovery on paper. As Thornton says: 'Had the great Victorian travellers not written anything, it would not be said today that they had "discovered" anything' (1983: 509).

Thornton points out how neatly Conrad captures the significance of the written narrative for the European experience of Africa in *Heart of Darkness* (1902). When the narrator finally tracks down Kurtz, who is the white man in the dark interior, he learns something of significance:

I learned that most appropriately, the international society for the suppression of savage customs had entrusted him with the making of a report, for its future guidance. And he had written it too. I've seen, I've read it. It was eloquent, vibrating with eloquence . . . it gave me the notion of an exotic Immensity ruled by an august benevolence. It made me tingle with enthusiasm. (Conrad, 1902, quoted in Thornton, 1983: 509)

Tingling with enthusiasm is not the response which reading ethnography normally produces in people. However, what is interesting about this passage is the terms in which the report is referred to. The report itself seems to be, as it were, more significant than the customs and peoples it describes. It is as if it is something more than a representation of Africa. It seems as if it is Africa. And more real for the European than the landscape and people themselves. Hence the ecstatic 'I've seen, I've read it. It was eloquent, vibrating with eloquence'. Somehow the experience is not possible without the text, that is, without the mediation of the text. Thornton says part of it:

More than a discovery, however, writing is a bridge that connects the limited context of speech and experience of primitive society to the larger world through the narrative that captures the experience of the particular and makes it available to a universal scrutiny. A new kind of understanding becomes at least possible . . . the ethnographic monograph, and other genres shaped around similar content . . . provide the crucial communicative link between cultures and between audiences that is the hallmark of anthropology. (1983: 510)

Thornton, I think, intends us to take this communicative link seriously, and to acknowledge the possibly emancipatory effects of this aspect of anthropological endeavour. I intend this communicative link ironically because it is in the attempt to establish a link between cultures and audiences that much of the problematic nature of anthropological authorship resides.

Thornton's analysis of the importance of the written narrative for the European experience of Africa is only part of the story, for he fails to explain why Conrad's narrator should tingle with enthusiàsm, why he should feel that the report speaks so directly to him. Here, I think, we encounter the relationship of narrative to desire. For the narrator, the report interprets Africa in terms of his own understandings of the purpose of Europeans, and therefore his own purpose, in being in Africa. It reveals something to him not about the landscape and the peoples of Africa, but about the land-scape of the European imagination in Africa. It makes sense, simultaneously, of the practical activities in which he and others are engaged, and of his fantasies about what he and others are doing in Africa. The activities of the individual and the imaginings of self come together in the text in a way which eludes the narrator in a day-to-day context.[3] It is this very function which anthropological texts so often perform for their authors and for their audiences, and it is for this reason that we cannot hope ever to come to any under-standing of these texts, or of the politics of their construction, unless we start by examining the relationship between authors and readers which is established in anthropological texts.

In order to explain this statement, and in order to explain why the new ethnography has made so little impact on the acceptability or otherwise of canonical writing in anthropology, it is necessary to begin by examining some aspects of the problematic nature of anthropological authorship. A number of critics have pointed out that the distinguishing mark of the anthropologist as author is the claim to possess an authentic experience. This experience is, of course, the product of having been there. Like all claims to authentic experience, the anthropologist's claim is difficult to assess. As Clifford Geertz points out, it gives much anthropological writing a kind of take-it-or-leave-it quality (1988: 5). It creates also a particular problem for the anthropologist who must produce a scientifically validated text out of a unique personal experience (Clifford, 1988: 26).

While no one seriously endeavours at the present time to model the social sciences on the natural sciences, the fact remains that for the vast majority of anthropologists it is still axiomatic that the society described in the text should be the society which the text claims to describe, and not some other. There must be some corre-spondence in 'good faith' between the anthropologist's interpret-ations of people's lives and the lives which those people actually lead. If we are going to agree that all cultural constructions, includ-ing anthropological descriptions and interpretations, are partial truths, historically and politically situated, then we must recognize that as far as many anthropologists are concerned anthropology's partial truths cannot be the same sort of partial truths as those displayed on our cinema screens and in contemporary fiction. One possible response to this dilemma is simply to say that in the contemporary context anthropology does not have a monopoly, if it ever did, of the interpretation of culture and of the discourse on difference. This means that anthropologists can carry on doing anthropology – an activity defined by specific sets of practices and forms of writing – but that they cannot claim any primacy for their interpretations over the interpretation of others (Clifford, 1988: 22, 52–4). Once the claim to primacy goes, then so does much of the anxiety. There is very little likelihood of immediate consensus on this issue either inside or outside the discipline. However, what the debate demonstrates is that the relationship between experience and text is still highly problematic and, although that relationship may be changing in response to the criticisms of the 'new ethnographers', the problem is simply displaced and not resolved.

The primacy of the anthropologist's interpretations of what was then termed 'native life' was not assured until the turn of the century – at least this is the story according to current narratives of the historical development of anthropology as a discipline. Before that moment, as I have briefly indicated, travellers, missionaries and administrators who had been 'in the field' a long time and had good linguistic skills were serious rivals (Clifford, 1988: 26). What is more, men like John Roscoe moved easily from one mode of communication or genre of writing to another. He wrote missionary accounts and he wrote scientific ethnography, and, in so doing, he moved from extensive use of the first person to a disembodied narrative voice, designed to convey objective neutrality (Thornton, 1983: 506–7). The interesting point, then, as a number of anthropologists have pointed out, is that the so-called Malinowskian revolution, where anthropology became characterized in the 1920s by long periods of research in the field, involving participant-observation, was not actually quite the revolution it was once thought to be. Many others had been living in other societies, making systematic observations, speaking the local language and writing about their findings long before Malinowski. It seems more likely that the revolution which Malinowski ushered in was not so much a revolution of method as a revolution in writing, in representation. What Malinowski insisted upon and what became the norm – in fact, the requirement of professional acceptance in anthropology, which it

remains to this day – was that anthropology should be a comparative science, and that the job of the anthropologist was to derive
theory from first-hand research. Prior to Malinowski there were
men on the spot (travellers, missionaries, administrators) who had
extensive knowledge which they wrote about, but their work was
not informed by scientific hypotheses; and there were the armchair
theorists, like Frazer, who wove grand comparative theories, but
who never visited the field (Kuper, 1973; Ellen, 1981; Stocking, 1983;
Clifford, 1988: 26–9). Malinowski's anthropologist was envisaged,
therefore, as having a new authority – a new professionalism and a
new method – and in order to convey this new authority what was
needed was a new form of writing. This authority was problematic
from the very beginning because while the research was to be based
on the in-depth field experience of the anthropologist, the writer of
the ethnographic monograph, who was one and the same person,
had to convince their audience that the facts before them were not
subjective creations, but objective pieces of information.

To establish the authority of the anthropologist as an author, two
kinds of authorial move within the text were required. The first was
that the author should appear and make a great deal of having been
there; and the second was that the author should then promptly
disappear, so as not to impugn the status of what was to follow.
These two strategies in anthropological writing are now well recognized and have been much discussed. However, I would like to
consider some of the stylistic strategies employed to pull off this
trick in early ethnographies, not because I want to cover familiar
ground, but so that I can use them as a starting point for developing
a rather different critique of anthropological writing from the one
that we normally find in the work of James Clifford, George Marcus,
Paul Rabinow and others.

The ethnographies of the 1920s and 1930s have much in common
with other forms of creative writing. The importance of travelling
to another place to experience it and the role of journeying or
travelling in the Romantic imagination can be seen clearly at work
in the writings of anthropologists. Much modern ethnography
shows strong, and unsurprising, parallels with travel writing, and
the shifts from first-person narration to generalized statement
which are characteristic of travel writing, right up to the present
day, are evident in anthropological writing (Pratt, 1986, 1992: 78).
Typically, the most obvious parallels occur in the opening passages

of the ethnography, when the writers are most concerned to establish the fact that they have been there, and that therefore they have the authority to speak.

> In the cool of the early morning, just before sunrise, the bow of the Southern Cross headed towards the eastern horizon, on which a tiny dark blue outline was faintly visible. Slowly it grew into a rugged mountain mass, standing up sheer from the ocean . . . in an hour or so we were close inshore, and could see canoes coming round from the south . . . The outrigger-fitted craft drew near, the men in them bare to the waist, girdled with bark-cloth, large fans stuck in the backs of their belts, tortoise-shell rings or rolls of leaf in the ear-lobes and nose, bearded, and with long hair flowing loosely over their shoulders . . . Almost before the chain was down the natives began to scramble aboard, coming over the side by any means that offered, shouting fiercely to each other and to us in a tongue of which not a word was understood by the mota-speaking folk of the mission vessel. I wondered how such turbulent human material could ever be induced to submit to scientific study. (Firth, [1936] 1957: 1–2)

The above passage is part of the first two pages of Raymond Firth's *We, the Tikopia* published in 1936. This passage is in no way unusual, and there are many others from anthropological writings of the period which could be used to make the same point. In many such passages there is a preference for break of day scenarios. One must, after all, begin at the beginning, mark a break with what has gone before, start the narrative moving forward. The metaphor of travel is important in many ethnographies, including many written in recent years. The travel metaphor sustains both the journey of the anthropologist, from home to abroad, from the familiar to the foreign, from ignorance to knowledge, and the journey of the reader which traverses much the same ground. The metaphor of travel often sustains also the theoretical discourse of the ethnography simply by incorporating it into the narrative, and thereby making it more comprehensible. There are other things happening, however, in these texts redolent with metaphors of travel, and these have to do with the topography of selves and others.

While early anthropology was influenced by travel writing, it was also influenced by the Victorian 'boy's own' story, in which the central theme is a heroic white man penetrating a dark continent at great personal risk: Rider Haggard's *King Solomon's Mines*, John Buchan's *Prester John* and many others. Anthropological imaginative discourse drew both on Romantic themes about the noble savage in Paradise and on the heroic quests of the adventure story genre. This duality is in evidence in the passage quoted earlier from Raymond Firth's book, and the fact that Firth may have intended his readers to read the passage ironically in no way undermines the general point. Discovery, adventure and difference are mixed in a most seductive fashion. Anyone with the misfortune to be familiar with the cultural genre involved can hear, on reading such descriptions, all the sounds, tones and colours of an imaginative childhood, enlarged to fill an adult world. There is absolutely nothing surprising about this, since the employment of a particular narrative form, bound together with familiar images and metaphors, was an obvious necessity for an anthropological discourse desirous of making itself intelligible. There was, in a sense, no alternative to these forms of writing because these were the forms of discourse available to anthropology to handle the relationship between self and other, sameness and difference. To have stood outside these forms of discourse – even supposing such a thing were possible – would have been a guarantee of unintelligibility. Even when writing ironically, the anthropologist as author would have had no alternative but to utilize these forms of discourse. The anthropological imagination, like any other imagination, is a thoroughly textualized one.

But the anthropological imagination of the 1930s and 1940s was a divided one, and often in conflict with itself. On the one hand, anthropologists wanted to hark back to Romantic ideas about the noble savage freed from the fetters of European control and the anti-slavery literature of the nineteenth century (Pratt, 1986). They often saw themselves as engaged in preserving alternative life-ways through recording them, and they were deeply concerned to make it plain that however different other people are, we all share a common humanity, a common capacity for rational thought and a common set of needs, strategies and motivations for living. On the other hand, the desire to develop anthropology as a comparative science of 'mankind' drew on the thoroughly Victorian images of quest, adventure and control. 'I wondered', wrote Firth, 'how such turbulent human material could ever be induced to submit to scientific study.'

What emerges from these considerations is that there is much ambiguity in the relationship of anthropology to its 'subject matter', an ambiguity which draws on, but does not totally overlap with the overdetermined and historically constituted relationship between the West and the Rest, and between colonizer and colonized. However, the ambiguities, divisions and conflicts in the anthropological imaginative discourse actually arise from a much more complex, three-dimensional figure, one which both constitutes and is constituted by the anthropologist as author. One dimension is certainly that provided in the relationship of domination and exploitation between colonizer and colonized. A second dimension concerns the relationship between the individual anthropologist and the people she studies. The third dimension concerns the relationship between the many selves of each individual self, its other selves. These three dimensions are implicated in and implicate each other. Properly speaking, therefore, they are not simply three dimensions, but many multiples of three. The management of such multiplicity is the central concern of anthropological writing. It is, in short, the problem of anthropological authorship.

The relationship between 'self' and 'other' in modern ethnography has a distinctive mark and that mark is the desirability and the fear of 'going native'. Going native, as many have remarked, is essential if one is to carry out participant-observation correctly, if one is to acquire that level of familiarity and identity on which good anthropological writing is supposed to be based. But it is to be avoided if one wants to write theoretical, comparative anthropology, if one wants to retain one's professional credentials and if one wants to safeguard one's sense of self. Going native is ultimately a fear about the erasure of difference, and in that erasure the loss of self. The self constitutes and defines itself through the 'detour of the other', and for this process to take place the other must exist and, if it does not exist, it must be created. Crudely put, stable selves require stable others. The instability of self and other accounts for the sense of vulnerability and panic which characterizes anthropological fieldwork for many anthropologists, and which is much talked about in the discipline and is represented in confessional writing.

Anthropologists are in the game, then, of creating the illusion of stable selves through which to view stable others, a necessity forced on them not only by the demands of a comparative science, but by the dictates of self-identity and self-preservation. Dictates, which I may say, are both culturally and historically specific. One way in which the relationship between selves and others is managed is through the creation of an authorial 'I' who authors the text. All the literary devices and strategies used to create the illusion of authority in the text have been widely discussed and analysed: the disembodied narrative voice, alternating with the use of the appearing and disappearing first person 'I' to mark the text through with the authentic experience; the attribution of stable sets of beliefs, attitudes and activities to coherent bodies or cultures, as in 'The Nuer believe that . . .'; and the use of free indirect speech to mask the arbitrary and precarious nature of individual interpretation, and to erase the fact that the researcher is always part of the research situation, as in, for example, 'Through sacrifice, the Nuer make a bargain with their God.' However, what is confusing about much so-called post-modernist analysis in anthropology is that it often appears to suggest that this organizing 'I', this authorial voice, is unproblematic. While it is agreed that this authorial voice is duplicitous, if not downright mendacious, it is assumed that what an analysis of rhetorical devices in the text does is to reveal the strategies, intentions and meanings of the author. This assumes, of course, an isomorphism between the 'I', the author created in the text, and the 'I', the individual who writes the text. This is revealed most dramatically, strangely enough, when post-modernist anthropologists come to talk, or rather write, about what the purpose of the new experimental ethnography would be, and what it would look like.

The first point about experimental ethnography is that it is concerned to make sure that the anthropologist is put back into the text as part of the research process, and that the experience of research, and its fundamentally interpersonal, communicative nature, should be revealed as the basis, and the only basis, for anthropological interpretations. The net result, as Geertz points out (1988: 97), is that we often end up with author saturated texts. There is a heavy irony here, because the more radical and experimental anthropology gets, and the more anthropologists are supposed to be seriously engaged in dispersing or sharing the authority of authorship with others, the more we are in danger of hearing about the anthropologist at the expense of hearing about others.[4] However, these author saturated texts necessarily and obviously presuppose that the author in the text and the author of the text are one and the same. Furthermore, even if we examine what many anthropologists see as the more radical proposals put forward by the new ethnography, namely the proposals for multiply authored texts, where dialogue, if not heteroglossia, is the organizing form (in so far as post-modernist texts are permitted to have any organizing form), we see that what is proposed is far from radical. This is because the multiplicity of voices and the multiple number of authors proposed for these texts would not in fact revise the standard anthropological notion of authorship, of what it is to author something, it would simply make it plural. In other words, the authors in the text would still be isomorphic in some way with the authors of the text, whoever those individuals might be. A further political dimension adds weight to the desire for identity between the authors in the text and the authors of the text: in a contemporary world where there is little sign that the combined forces of neo-imperialism and international capitalism are on the wane there is every reason to argue that anthropology must faithfully represent the realities and complexities of communication and discussion between historically situated individuals. We must not invent characters in our dramas.

It is an irony of the contemporary moment that while international capitalism and other forces threaten homogeneity, difference is on the political agenda more than ever. Anthropology thus retains an anxiety about the charge of fictionalization. This may be a displaced anxiety, but is nevertheless there. It is, of course, the political realization of the fact that global systems of domination are embedded in discourses of difference and in the representation of others which draws post-modernist anthropology into a situation where it imagines that the answer to anthropology's crisis of representation – which is actually a political crisis – is to develop a form of text in which a number of individuals have their say, and in which a number of perspectives and points of view are put forward. This may be exactly what happens in the fieldwork situation, in the context of interpersonal exchange, but the desire for a text which somehow faithfully represents this fieldwork situation is doomed to disappointment. It is doomed to disappointment because the relationship between the author in the text and the author of the text is not a direct and straightforward one. It is not straightforward because it is imaginary; it is fictive in the sense that it is arbitrary and symbolic, set up in language and culturally inscribed. When I say that the relationship between these two authors – the individual who signs the text and the 'I' or organizing subject created in the text – is fictive and imaginary, I do not mean to imply that these authors have nothing to do with each other, no real connection. I mean simply that the one is the imaginary self of the other. Properly speaking, they are not two selves, but a self in process.

If we accept the post-structuralist, post-modernist argument that the unitary, rational subject is an historical product and not a universal category and if we stress that individuals construct a sense of self, a subjectivity, through a variety of subject positions provided in discursive practices, some of which may be mutually contradictory, then we can begin to make an argument about the necessity, albeit under specific cultural and discursive conditions, of constructing a sense of self, a unitary coherent self, that can act in the world. One way in which this unitary, coherent self is constructed is through the representation of self or selves in text. Anthropologists do not just represent their experience of an 'other' culture in the text, they also constitute and produce their experience and themselves in the text. The constitution of self is a labour, it is work, and it is imaginary. It is achieved symbolically, through language and, in this case, through the mediation of the text. The process of textualization is one of the major ways in which anthropologists assign meaning to their experiences and give them value. The 'I' or organizing subject in the text is the fictively created, unitary self which guarantees the authentic experience and thus the verisimilitude of the cultural representation the text contains. It is a magical trick and exceptionally difficult to pull off.

When Geertz says that Vincent Crapanzano's experimental ethnography *Tuhami* (1980) turns an evocative homage of the other into a self-fulfilling homage to the self, he comes close to making a similar point (1988: 90–6). Crapanzano discusses the life of Tuhami, a Moroccan tile-maker, and he connects what he experiences and what Tuhami tells him to Lacan, Freud, Nietzsche, Kierkegaard, d'Annunzio, Simmel, Sartre, Blanchot, Heidegger, Hegel, Genet, Gadamer, Schutz, Dostoevsky, Jung, Frye and Nerval. There are, apparently, striking parallels between Nerval and Tuhami. It is evident that all these great men have much of import to say regarding the nature of the human condition, and in that sense it seems quite likely that their writings could be relevant to an understanding of anyone's life. However, we are not learning about Tuhami here, we are learning about Crapanzano. But this is much more than the comprehension of the self by the 'detour of the other', this is the imaginary constitution of self, the desire to make sense of self through assigning value and meaning to experience, the desire to capture a complete self which then becomes knowable. This is a work of extraordinary synthesis, and what is constructed in it is not Tuhami, but Crapanzano. Crapanzano is aware of this fact (see also Crapanzano, 1992). For one thing, anthropology has long been very clear that the purpose of cross-cultural comparison is not just the study of 'them', but the equally important study of 'us' – whoever 'us' might be – though this has conventionally been taken to mean the study of 'our' cultural beliefs, concepts, attitudes and behaviours, and not the study of ourselves as selves. But, Crapanzano is aware of the deeper irony, mentioned earlier, that the more the anthropologist seems to undo the authorial strategies of anthropological writing, to unmask the constructed nature of anthropological interpretations and to examine their negotiated and contested nature, the more anthropological writing must engage with these issues, and as it becomes more self-conscious and self-critical, it expands to fill the page. The anthropological self is more in evidence than ever.

The process of constructing self through the process of textualization has much to do with the function of narrative. It has been argued by Hayden White and Paul Ricoeur and many others that narrative is a strategy for placing us within an historically constituted world, and thus our very concept of history is dependent on narrative. If narrative makes the world intelligible, it also makes ourselves intelligible.

> What is involved in the discovery of the 'true story' within or behind the events that come to us in the chaotic form of 'historical records'? What wish is enacted, what desire is gratified, by the fantasy that real events are properly represented when they can be shown to display the formal coherence of a story? In the enigma of this wish, this desire, we catch a glimpse of the cultural function of narrativising discourse. (White, 1978: 8, quoted in De Lauretis, 1984)

Desire and narrative are thus enmeshed, and this enmeshing allows us to start unpacking the anthropologist as author. I take as the starting point for what follows the work of Teresa de Lauretis. I do not claim to say anything that she has not already said much more brilliantly, except perhaps in so far as these issues pertain to anthropological writing. De Lauretis, like others, sees narrative as a fundamental way of making sense of the world. She argues that the structure of narrative offers readers a limited set of positions within the plot space. To receive pleasure from the text, each reader must assume the 'positionalities of meaning and desire' made available by the text.[5] For the period that the reader assumes those positions, their subjectivity is 'engaged in the cogs of narrative and indeed constituted in the relation of narrative, meaning and desire, so that the very work of narrativity is the engagement of the subject in certain . . . positionalities of meaning and desire'(De Lauretis, 1984: 196). For the reader, the text binds fantasy and affect to certain images and metaphors. The historical and ideological nature of these images and metaphors means that although the text powerfully participates in the production of forms of subjectivity which are individually shaped, these forms of subjectivity are also unequivocally social (De Lauretis, 1984: 37). The anthropological monograph is a text which constructs images or visions of social reality. But this text is involved in the production and reproduction of meanings, values and ideology at both the social and the subjective level. The anthropological monograph is thus a work which produces effects of meaning and perception, self-images and subject positions, and it does so for both readers *and* authors.

The question is that if subjectivity is constituted for both readers and authors through taking up the subject positions provided by the narrative, then what induces them to assume these positions (see chapter 3)? De Lauretis deals with this question by using the concept of identification. In order for a narrative to work, it has to please. Pleasure can simply be something of interest, whether it is aesthetic or theoretical or ethnographic. Anthropologists love knowing about new pieces of ethnography, especially when these new items are offered in the adventurous style of much anthroplogical narrative! Pleasure depends on a personal response, an engagement of the reader's subjectivity, and this offers the possibility of identification. This process of identification is particularly important in anthropological writing where the reader is being encouraged to identify strongly with the author, or rather with the positions that the author takes up in the text. The desire involved or implicated in the narrative is the desire to know, to see, to receive pleasure, and the narrative shapes and contains that desire.

The situation is more complex, however, because readers can read a text. They can read 'against the grain' of the text. They may recognize also the way the narrative is shaping and constraining interpretive possibilities. Indeed, they may recognize or apprehend the way the narrative shapes and continues their own desire, and they may resist this, dissenting from the text. But resistance, dissent and even criticism require, as has often been argued, prior recognition. In fact, they are all critically dependent on such recognition. The multiplicity of subject positions proffered by the text means that identification can be partial, temporary and changing. There is no need to imagine that all readers will identify with all the positions proffered in the text, nor is there any reason to assume that the process of identification is without contradiction and conflict. Many of the subject positions in the text will actually be contradictory and inconsistent (see chapter 3).

The fact that anthropological texts address readers both as individuals and as members of a social group implies that certain patterns or possibilities of identification for all readers must be built into the text (De Lauretis, 1984: 136). These patterns or possibilities of identification are directly related to the intelligibility of the text. It is for this reason that anthropological writing appears so wedded to conventional narrative form, and to images and metaphors, like the metaphor of journeying, which allow readers not only to identify, but to indulge in the pleasure of anticipation. The pleasure for the author is also in the familiar form of the narrative, in the pleasure of a story well told according to the conventions of narrative, in the investment in making it come out right, in the success of having described another culture, written a book and pulled it all off without anyone realizing that one was somehow not quite up to it. It is for all these reasons that the author creates certain positions of meaning and desire, which not only engage their subjectivity, but also engage the subjectivity of their readers in a way which will permit a considerable degree of identification between author and reader.

The identification so desired works, however, on a number of levels. The author *of* the text wishes to identify with the author *in* the text, the unitary, complete self, who has successfully done the fieldwork and written the text and is the hero of the tale. The author

of the text also wants the reader to identify with them, through
assuming that the author *in* the text is isomorphic with the author *of*
the text. We all want to be the heroes of our own stories, and there
is just enough of the intrepid traveller left in the popular image of
the anthropologist to allow anthropologists to construct themselves
in that image. We may no longer be heroic voyagers, but we are not
above swapping stories about who had the most horrible time in the
field and trading details of life-threatening tropical diseases. And
even if we are too sophisticated to go in for such transparent self-
aggrandizement, we find it hard to resist congratulating ourselves
on our self-critical, self-reflective, post-colonial stance. There are
many ways to play the hero. The reader *of* the text wants to identify
with the author *in* the text, or rather to identify with the positions of
meaning and desire which the author takes up and makes available
to the reader. To be pleasurable, the process of identification does
not have to be complete and it can incorporate, as I have suggested,
and very often does, a component of resistance or dissent. Finally,
the reader *of* the text wants to identify with the author *of* the text
through the medium of the author *in* the text. We all like to imagine
ourselves as someone else, or at least as the equivalent of someone
else, especially if that someone is successful or seems desirable in
other ways. There are many other forms of identification which
could be discussed, but with regard to the question of the identification between author and reader consider the following passage,
which James Clifford has made famous as an exemplar of conventional anthropological writing, albeit for purposes rather different
from mine (1988: 33).

> It is difficult to find an English word that adequately describes the
> social position of dil in a tribe. We have called them aristocrats, but
> do not wish to imply that Nuer regard them as of superior rank, for,
> as we have emphatically declared, the idea of a man lording it over
> others is repugnant to them. On the whole – we will qualify the
> statement later – the dil have prestige rather than rank and influence
> rather than power. If you are a dil of the tribe in which you live you
> are more than a simple tribesman. You are one of the owners of the
> country, its village sites, its pastures, its fishing pools and wells.
> Other people live there by virtue of marriage into your clan, adoption
> into your lineage, or of some other social tie. You are a leader of the
> tribe and the spear-name of your clan is invoked when the tribe goes
> to war. Whenever there is a dil in the village, the village clusters

around him as a herd around its bull. (Evans-Pritchard, [1940] 1969: 215)

This is a passage from Evans-Pritchard's *The Nuer* (published in 1940), one of the great canonical texts of British social anthropology. There are a number of rhetorical devices at work in the passage. First, the reader is identified, through elision, with the author in the text: 'We have called them aristocrats.' Then the reader is identified with the Nuer: 'If you are a dil of the tribe in which you live you . . .' The passage also contains all the marks of authentic experience in the familiarity it implies the anthropologist has with Nuer ideas and customs; and it also carries with ease the burden of the objective, scientific gaze in the guise of a typical event: 'Whenever there is a dil in the village . . .' Sameness and difference are woven into this passage in ways which demonstrate what a past master Evans-Pritchard really was of the genre. The difficulties of translation referred to in the first sentence imply difference, but are presented in a way which also suggests the anthropologist's familiarity with this knowable, if not yet completely specified, other (Clifford, 1988: 33–4). This familiarity carries forward into the rest of the passage where the subtle nuances of status and rank are described as if they were part of the English class system. The reader is being encouraged to identify with an aristocratic class among the Nuer, and being encouraged to do so by an anthropologist whose own familiarity with the importance and subtlety of rank and status marks him as someone who appreciates these things. It is a truly masterful piece of writing. It is seductive, it is engaging, and it has just that *frisson* of sexuality and power which caused Conrad's narrator to tingle with enthusiasm: 'You are a leader of the tribe and the spear-name of your clan is invoked when the tribe goes to war. Whenever there is a dil in the village, the village clusters around him as a herd around its bull.' This passage employs in recognizable ways the discourse on self and other which is characteristic of many genres of writing. The Nuer referred to in the text in the present tense are a stable, changeless and typified entity which act as a permanent foil for English identity and English selves.[6] However, it is also quite clear that these abstracted Nuer are male, and that the anthropologist and the reader are male also.

The predominant metaphors in anthropological writing and the prominent practices in terms of the activity of anthropology – participant-observation, systematic data collection, cultural description – all imply a process of looking at, examining, 'objectifying' and 'collecting'. This visualism is manifest in most anthropological writing, especially in the constant use of *mise en scène* techniques which writers use to convey the authentic nature of the anthropologist's experience and their description (Clifford and Marcus, 1986: 11–12). This means that it is the act of observation which is repeatedly represented in the text, and this effectively makes the reader, in one way or another, the accomplice of a voyeur (Minh-ha, 1989: 69). The voyeurism, the act of looking, is the act of othering. The people who are studied and examined begin under the gaze of the anthropologist, but as the narrative develops they are increasingly specified, brought under the control of the anthropologist, and become the property of the anthropologist. They become in the end an extension of the male self, its other looking back at it, reflecting it at 'twice its normal size'. The male and female discussed here do not, of course, refer directly or straightforwardly to individual men and women. This is clearly the case, since many people studied by anthropologists are male, and their 'feminization' through the process of objectification and the assumption of the position of other in relation to the male self still proceeds.

In similar vein, we have the problem of the woman anthropologist, and the woman reader of the anthropological text. The straightforward response to this is simply to say that the processes of identification under discussion are not the unproblematic outcome of the known gender identity of historical individuals. Identification is not single or simple. Identification is a relation, part of the process of becoming a subject, and it involves the identification of oneself with something other than oneself, so that subjectivity is constituted through a series of such identifications (De Lauretis, 1984: 141). Women anthropologists and women readers identify with the desiring subject, the hero, and they simultaneously identify with that hero's other, with his object of desire. Women readers and authors are able to take up and partially identify, at best partially, with the male position in the text, with those positions which are given particular value and meaning; and in so doing they construct a sense of self, a self which is imaginary. Subjectivity is social and historical as well as individual, and therefore through the process of identification one acquires a social as well as an individual subjectivity. Women anthropologists and women readers do not float free of their social and historical contexts, of the particular discourses available to them for the construction of self. To be successful anthropologists, women have to identify with the valorized male position. They are also historical beings and they cannot necessarily stand outside the discourses available to them for constructing relations between self and other.

This may be one reason why, until very recently, there was very little which was distinctive about the writing of women anthropologists. The tension between objectifying gaze and authentic experience is there, the rhetorical devices for establishing authorial authority are there. However, the process of identification is never complete, never perfect or finished. The writing of women anthropologists is not actually the same as that of their male colleagues. With the notable exception of Margaret Mead, women anthropologists, like Audrey Richards, Lucy Mair, Monica Wilson and Phyllis Kaberry – all of whom did fieldwork in the 1930s and 1940s – do not use the 'as I was standing under the palm tree' approach to ground their authentic experience. They avoid the travel writing style and the metaphors of journeying. Their overall style is often very distant and slightly cold. They aim, perhaps, for a markedly scientific status in their writing, and thus it often lacks the evocative detail of their male colleagues. This is no doubt, in part, because they were under particular pressure to demonstrate their scientific abilities and professional rigorousness, being prone to lapses in objectivity and to subjective interpretation on account of their gender! But it is also, in part, that they seem to have more difficulty in constructing that easy familiarity with the other which is part of the process of creating a unitary male self, an imaginary self who acts as the organizing consciousness of the text. The imaginary male author *in* the text eludes the female author *of* the text and the woman anthropologist retreats into objectivity and distance to cover over this lack. This may be one reason why women anthropologists are so often accused of writing very boring ethnography.[7]

The questions, then, at this stage are, is the post-modernist turn going to offer anthropology any hope? Will it provide it with sufficient grounds for self-reflection in the endless process of meaning deferred to work against its historical role in the discourses and practices of domination? Will the new experimental anthropology provide modes of shared authorship, shifting perspectives and fragmented domains of partially shared cultural meanings in a way which will allow other people to speak alongside the anthropologist, from within the same text, in a manner direct, equal and independent? Have we grounds for anticipating the imminent demise of the traditional anthropological author?

There are as yet very few post-modernist texts in anthropology; one, however, which has received much acclaim is Michael Taussig's *Shamanism, Colonialism and the Wild Man*. As we might expect, Taussig is against traditional anthropological modes of authorizing and authenticating texts. He inserts himself into his discourse, and he builds up the argument using refraction, displacement and the repetition of powerful images. This seems a truly decentred and deconstructed text, full of shifts, fragmentation and polyphony. But more than one unkind reviewer has remarked that the average professional anthropologist, never mind the average person, finds it almost impossible to comprehend this text precisely because there is no story to follow. In a text of this kind, as Kapferer (1988) has so cogently pointed out, the idea is that the author builds up images and metaphors one on top of the other, capturing the sense of a complex, shifting reality, so that the 'facts' can speak for themselves. The authority of the anthropologist as author is decentred. The problem, of course, is that the facts do not speak for themselves, and this carnivalesque form of empiricism gives very little meaning or import to the experience of the anthropologist or to the experiences of people living in Colombia. In spite of Taussig's professed antagonism to traditional modes of anthropological writing, he frequently uses *mise en scène* techniques.

> From the vantage point of his house by the river in the foothills beyond the sugar plantations and the great groaning mass of humanity sustaining them, Don Benito can afford to be a little snooty. 'Nothing but pig sties' he says of the sugar cane towns, rural slums one and all, created by the new agribusiness systems. 'Pure filth' he exclaims. And by filth he means sorcery. (Taussig, 1986: 274)

Don Benito no more speaks for himself in this context than he might have done in one produced by Malinowski. He is still represented as representative, and we are being encouraged to understand or comprehend Don Benito by visualizing him. This passage is in no way atypical of the book as a whole. However, the more important point concerns the argument about the dispersion of the anthropologist's authorial authority. It is not just that he can be seen setting the scene, as in the above quotation. Consider the following passage:

> In his uncompleted manuscript on commodity fetishism and the modern European city, Walter Benjamin wrote that 'in the dream which every epoch sees it images the epoch which is to succeed it, the latter appears coupled with elements of prehistory – that is to say classless society'. Certainly, there was a passion for classlessness among one set of 'prehistoric elements' in the modern agribusiness town of Puerto Tejada, and that was the large grouping of black migrants from the trackless jungles of the Pacific Coast'. (Taussig, 1986: 282)

Whose dream are we in here, whose reality is this or whose illusion of reality is this? The association of European thought with the experiences of black migrant workers is cavalier rather than illuminating; such an association can be understood only as an attempt to make sense of a European self. Taussig's concern with decentring and deconstruction in the text looks very like a reworking of a metropolitan crisis in the context of Colombia. Long passages in this book read like scenes from *Apocalypse Now*, the imaginative reworking of the nightmare of Vietnam (Kapferer, 1988). This is the context in which we should be reading this text. These are the metaphors and images which are replacing the images of travel and the metaphors of journeying. Perhaps the chaotic, fragmented nature of the relationship between order and disorder which the shamans of Colombia manage means that they are true deconstructionists, or perhaps it means that they are the other selves of the anthropologist, working in the text to produce his imaginary self.

It seems that the dispersion and fragmentation of authorial authority and even of the authors themselves are not really about a change in anthropological authorship, that is, in the nature of the anthropologist as author. They have more to do with changing concepts of the self, and most especially the anthropological self. The definition of the anthropological hero has changed. We are no longer objective, comparative scientists, but self-reflexive, self-critical, connected individuals. This newly valorized subject position is no less male than the one which preceded it, and its liberal credentials should be viewed with the same scepticism.[8]

However, there have been significant changes in the genres and styles of anthropological writing. As anthropologists and as authors, our imaginations are now textualized and contextualized very differently from the way they were for anthropologists writing in the 1940s, 1950s and 1960s. The sources of our images and metaphors are different and the images and metaphors themselves have altered. The changes in disciplinary fashions and the sheer volume of anthropological writing produced have provided us with a larger number of models on which to base our own writing as individuals, even if this process works through contradiction and dissent, as it does for many feminist anthropologists. There is now no single way to write anthropology. But even in our moments of greatest self-reflection there is very little sign that we have relinquished our authorial authority. We are just re-creating and rewriting our relationship with ourselves – our many selves – and with others. Our writing continues much in the image of ourselves, as must inevitably be the case if we are to establish any kinds of relations with others.

7

THE FEMINIST ANTHROPOLOGIST
AND THE PASSION(S) OF
NEW EVE

This essay is an anthropologist's look at the writings of a novelist. It is one producer of fictions' examination of the manner in which the fictions of another are crafted. This rather strange activity is inspired by a particular question, and that question is one about the context(s) of the imagination. There has been much talk recently in anthropology about the craft of writing, the process of constructing cultures and the making of other people's lives, as well as about the form in which these representations are served up for consumption. If we agree that modelling is both an imaginative and a symbolic activity, then we need to enquire into the context(s) of the anthropological imagination. Where do anthropologists get their models of society from?

Anthropological writing and the fictive category of 'the West'

In large part, of course, they get them from other anthropologists. This is one of the functions of a disciplinary training. It provides you with a language, a set of symbols and a *modus vivendi*. This applies as much to the practicalities of anthropological fieldwork as it does to the writing of ethnography. It is probably true to say that an anthropologist's disciplinary training provides her with a very special way of speaking about and relating to the world. This alternative 'world' is not, however, continuously present; it can be picked up and put down, almost at will. Rather like the theoretical physicist whose world is peopled – often quite literally – by quarks and black holes, except when she is playing the piano, for example, when such entities are pushed to the back of the mind. Compartmentalization of this kind probably prevents us all from going mad in a world which is far too full of knowledge. It also allows Nobel Prize winning scientists to be practising Muslims or Catholics, so that faith can co-exist with science. Anthropologists are no different, and they do believe in a number of imagined entities, like kinship systems, symbols and typologies. Mercifully, these imagined entities recede as soon as one boils an egg, says a prayer or collects a child from school. Normality is everyone's refuge. However, recent feminist critiques of science, as well as others, have pointed out that if our worlds are compartmentalized, they are only imperfectly so. The fact that we traffic back and forth across their borders means that they contaminate each other. More than this, they become not just intertwined, but interdependent.

Disciplinary training is not the only problem. Mary Douglas once remarked that one of the great misfortunes to befall people who are the subjects of anthropological enquiry is that they inevitably end up resembling the anthropologists who study them. Thus, the Nuer – studied by the British – turned out to be phlegmatic politicians, while the Dogon – studied by the French – are aesthetes with an interest in language and systems of signification. The refiguring of some people's lives in terms of the salient concerns of others is a perennial problem for anthropology (see, for example, Trinh Minh-ha, 1989, 1990; Mohanty, 1991; and Lazareg, 1988). The anthropological gaze risks turning subjects into objects; othering them in a permanent relation to an anthropological self which by virtue of disciplinary training and philosophical orientation, if by nothing else, is frequently a kind of quasi North American or European self. These imagined selves are part of the amorphous, non-sensical, but still powerful, category of the West. Anthropology, like many academic disciplines, often invokes something called the West in order to derive a series of working contrasts or differences. This entity is, of course, another imagined one.

One facet of the problem is that non-western anthropologists – and the term here obscures more than it reveals – often have to write about their findings in terms of the West versus the Rest dichotomy which informs theoretical concepts in the discipline. For example, a Japanese anthropologist who wants to work on concepts of the person or the self in Samoa may find herself having to describe such concepts in terms of implicit, international disciplinary conventions. She cannot begin with her personal concepts of the person or the self, nor indeed with those she might wish to label Japanese. She must, either implicitly or explicitly, orient at least part of her discussion in terms of the recognized debate within anthropology, and in so doing she brings into play the set of contrasted and contrastive differences which depend for their existence on the imagined category of the West. This is most particularly the case if the anthropologist is writing in English, or in one of the other European languages in which much of the international theoretical debate in the discipline takes place. This does not mean that the terrain of theoretical debate and the conventions of linguistic usage cannot be shifted – they can. But we should be clear about the intellectual and political implications of the hegemony of the 'them' versus 'us' division on which anthropology's notion of cultural difference depends.

What does the category of the West refer to? Is it co-terminous with a definitive group(s) of people? Can it be used as a coherent cultural category, as a backdrop against which anthropological practitioners can foreground alternative cultural models? There is an implicit assumption not only in critical anthropological discourse, but in cultural studies and colonial discourse theory that a coherent and hegemonic unified category called the West exists, and that it can be identified with specific people in specific times and places in some way or other.[1] We are not always sure exactly who these people are, but we presume they are white, sometimes male, and that they have some sort of connection with governance and ruling. What the existence of these implied co-ordinates amounts to is a failure to recognize that the West is an imagined category. This does not mean, of course, that we should deny or exclude the powerful material effects of the discursive and practical deployment of the West as a category – the things that have been done in its name, so to speak. The fragility and partiality of this discursively constructed 'West' are hidden from us in consequence of its own ideological effects. Who or what is the West? The answer is apparently a double negative: no one and nothing. Occasionally certain archetypal figures, like Margaret Thatcher or Ronald

Reagan, proffer themselves as the symbolic personification of that discursive space and thus trick us once again into thinking that it exists in some very straightforward and obvious sense.

But what do the people who make up this category 'the West' have to say about it? Do all the members of the category identify with it in the same way? For example, members of the British Asian and Afro-Caribbean communities might not readily identify with the category of the West as deployed in anthropology, cultural studies and colonial discourse theory; with that particular set of cultural values, symbols, social structures and ways of being shored up by acts of violence and economic opportunism. And yet, they so obviously are part of any sensible definition of the West; they are at the heart of the category, even as they seek to resist it, transform it and educate it. The fact that this was not always so, that the communities now at the centre were once at the periphery, is one of the most powerful material and discursive effects of the West. From this point of view it is clear that the West is not to be identified with people and places, symbols and values. It is rather a discursive space, a set of positionalities, a network of economic and political power relations, a domain of material and discursive effects.

The fact that the West cannot be simply identified with a concrete set of people with concrete beliefs means that few people who are of the West can be said to be its true representatives. Thus, to whom do anthropologists refer when they contrast the West with the Rest, 'us' with 'them'? Cultural beliefs attributed to the West are certainly not representative of the peoples of different class, colour, religion and nationality who make up the West. The guiding philosophical principles of western thought (such as the Cartesian split, the subject/object divide, the Enlightenment subject) all encode assumptions – about the nature of the world, the self in the world and about how knowledge of that world is acquired – that have probably never been subscribed to by the majority of westerners, whoever they may be and might have been (see chapter 2). Local discourses on the self and its relation to a lived world often have relatively little to do with the elite discourses of philosophy, religion and politics. Some would argue that education and democratization have made these discourses available to the mass of people. This is undoubtedly true, but it does not mean that people subscribe to these discourses, that they believe in them. To transmute a phrase of Clifford Geertz's: it does not mean that people find the concepts and categories produced in such discourses to be 'experience-near' ones. In fact, it seems that more often they are 'experience-far' ones; that is, they are of little help in comprehending the practical and sensate world of experience. Thus, we do not need information about quarks to play the piano or a knowledge of kinship to boil an egg. But, more importantly, we do not necessarily find that academic and/or expert discourses of various kinds help us to deal with daily life, and we often prefer to draw on local models and discourses. Consequently, we do not need to know anything about the anthropological analysis of kinship in order to have intimate relationships, though we almost certainly need some kind of model of a social life and one which comes into an approximate relation with our own beliefs about our lives.

Models of the world: academic and popular

This point has been at the basis of a good many theories in sociology and anthropology. But having said this, it is clear that academic and/or expert discourses of all kinds do filter into popular discourse in a variety of ways and become transformed in the process; sometimes they may even bring about change at the popular level. By way of example for the United Kingdom in the years since the Second World War, I would cite genetics, psychoanalysis and feminism. Everybody now knows about genes, but what they know about them is something else. Some people in the United Kingdom know that it is possible to inherit Huntington's chorea, but they also believe that one can inherit bad temper, blue blood and a number of other things. The recent focus in medical research on genetic propensity or predisposition has translated into popular discourse as destiny; it is as if popular theories of genetic inheritance provide moral answers for a secular age.[2]

Psychoanalysis has entered popular culture, in the UK at least, in a form which stresses the determining power of childhood experiences, an obsession with fathers and an anxiety about bad mothers. Not very much may be known about psychoanalytic theory, but a whole series of popular experiences – like motivation in crime novels and television dramas – has been profoundly influenced by theories of causation and personality development based on a version of psychoanalytic thought. It would not be an exaggeration to say that psychoanalysis has entered almost everyone's lived conception of self. Psychoanalytic discourse, or at least a popular version of it, has produced a situation where the scientific, the philosophical, the medical and the personal come into some kind of lived relation to each other. What is interesting about this is the way in which no one's view of psychoanalysis, or indeed of self, can ever be free again of this bowdlerized, popular version. This is true even of people who concern themselves with psychoanalysis as theorists and practitioners; and it is true also of anthropologists and feminists.

The question of how different discourses intertwine and over-determine each other, and of how the academic influences the popular and vice versa, is the main theme of this essay. My conten-tion is that what masquerade as academic models are often little more than popular discourses in disguise, or rather that the popular and the academic are overdetermined in ways that are not only very difficult to untangle, but absolutely essential for the workings of each. If we turn, for example, to look at the forms of popular culture which shape the context of the imagination for working feminists and anthropologists, it immediately becomes clear that these cul-tural productions do not deal in stable notions of person, self and gender. It is impossible, I would suggest, to come away from mod-ern fiction with the notion of a singular concept of the western person or self intact. For one thing, the impact of the writing of people of colour – poets, playwrights, novelists and scriptwriters – in the United Kingdom has long undermined any single stable notion of British self-identity. Fictional writing constantly reveals the search for such a self to be an imaginary one. Popular culture, in its myriad forms, works and reworks concepts of self, identity and gender into a kaleidoscope of possibilities. Some of these possi-bilities are informed by academic or intellectual discourses which have taken on popular forms, as in the cases of psychoanalysis and feminism. Yet other possibilities are influenced by local models and local experiences that are rarely, if ever, represented in dominant intellectual and academic discourses, even those, like feminism and anthropology, which are explicitly committed to representing such models. But, more importantly, I want to suggest that when anthro-pologists and feminists come to use intellectual or academic models, they are influenced in their interpretation of those models by popular versions of them made available through fiction and other means. And that this is so because it is through these popular versions that researchers are able to bring so-called intellectual models closer to their own self-experiences and self-understandings, and to explore their imaginative possibilities. The fictive works here to constitute the domain of the possible.

I want to explore this issue further by looking at one of the novels of Angela Carter, *The Passion of New Eve*. I chose this novel because of its subject matter; it is explicitly about sex, gender and sexual identity, amongst other things. It is also equally obviously a feminist novel, and as such it is an example of the overdetermination of academic and popular discourse.[3] However, its emphasis on representation and symbolism and its overt concern with social relations and the conditions of sociality make it also in some senses an anthropological novel. It is, I tentatively suggest, the kind of novel which has become possible precisely because of the manner in which anthropology and feminism have entered the domain of the popular. And I want to use my reading of it to indicate how the popular and the fictive provide the imaginative impetus for the academic models and discourses of feminism and anthropology.

The true context(s) of the anthropologist's imagination, or at least of the feminist anthropologist's imagination, can never simply be academic and anthropological. This is a point which might be hardly worth making were it not for the fact that these issues are rarely discussed. I would be prepared to lay a bet that if you asked an anthropologist in the United Kingdom where they got their inspiration from for their ethnographic writing, even a feminist anthropologist, they would probably say Audrey Richards or Evans-Pritchard or Margaret Mead or Malinowski. The question is, would this be true? One would hardly dare say that one was getting one's inspiration from Fay Weldon or Ntoshoke Shange or Margaret Atwood or June Jordan or Tsitsi Dangarembga or Jean Rhys. In the context that I know about, one could not even say that one was getting one's inspiration from George Eliot, lest one be thought pretentious.[4]

The other reason I have chosen Angela Carter has to do with the politics of positionality and specificity. Angela Carter died recently, and I am sure that if she were still alive she would be horrified to be reckoned into any degree of kinship or common view with me. I do not claim that I represent her or she me. However, in trying to situate the context of the anthropological and the feminist imaginations, I have to have regard for specifics. What sort of anthropologist or feminist, located where, writing about what? I share something with Angela Carter in terms of colour and class and geographical location, and the experience of the United Kingdom in the 1980s, and a knowledge of the British feminist movement and its debates. I do not share her apparent fascination with fairy tales and mythologies, with the Gothic and the fantastic, but perhaps I have had my imagination informed by many of the things which have informed hers. The assumptions of commonality here are very tenuous, but they are important. As I write in the following pages of 'the feminist anthropologist', I write of myself and, sometimes, by extension, of other feminist anthropologists operating within some kind of British context.[5]

Angela Carter and the passion(s) of new Eve

One very common assumption at the present time is that there are two sexes and two genders, and that there exists between them a set of rather obvious correspondences. The assertion that gender is not determined by sex has simply reinforced a division between the biological and the social in a way which leaves our understanding of biological sex fairly intact and very under-theorized (see chapters 1 and 2). Carter takes up this theme in *The Passion of New Eve* and actively seeks to parody and destabilize the relationship between sex and gender. She stresses the performative and surface nature of gender identity, and she does so by dealing with the question of bodily and sexual transformation at several different levels.

Eve, the anti-heroine of the tale, starts her narration as Evelyn, a young male English academic who leaves home to take a job in New York. Carter deliberately plays on stereotypes of British and American culture to portray this journey as a dangerous move into the unknown, but into an unknown of incredible seductive power. During the story Evelyn seduces and betrays a young black woman, Leilah, and leaves the city for the desert, where he is transformed by Mother, Goddess of all, into a beautiful young woman. Evelyn, newly born as Eve, escapes from the utopian underworld run by the devotees of Mother when she realizes that she is to be impregnated with her own sperm. Flight, however, only leads to further capture, and she falls into the clutches of the one-eyed, one-legged poet Zero.

After being raped by Zero, Eve lives as a member of his harem and joins him in his hunt for Tristessa, the retired movie-star who the poet believes has rendered him sterile through the screen display of her excessive femininity. Tristessa, as it happens, was the boyhood love object and heroine of Evelyn in her former male state. In the course of the narrative's denouement the beautiful Tristessa is herself revealed as a man, and a full reversal takes place when she, as he, enters Eve, once Evelyn, now physically transformed into his other.

One of the main themes in the book, and one which Carter reworks in several of her other novels, has to do with the way in which woman is constructed as man's other. If Carter represents the passivity and negativity of woman as sign, she also plays with the sexual economy of exchanges within this binary frame, and much of her sharpest writing is reserved for the way in which male subjectivity finds itself mirrored in women as woman. People invent themselves through inventing their other, and sometimes with disastrous consequences. When Evelyn betrays Leilah in the opening pages of the novel by getting her pregnant and then abandoning her, her weakness and his self-loathing are made equally apparent.

> She was a perfect woman; like the moon, she only gave reflected light. She had mimicked me, she had become the thing I wanted of her, so that she could make me love her and yet she had mimicked me so well she had also mimicked the fatal lack in me that meant I was not able to love her because I myself was so unlovable. (34)

Evelyn refers elsewhere to being infected by 'the sickness of femininity, its passivity, its narcissism' (37). The narcissistic self is, of course, the masculine self, constructed in relation to its feminine other. Carter plays most brutally on this fact by having Evelyn castrated and turned into his other self, Eve. But the imaginary nature of the desire involved in self-fashioning is revealed most starkly through the unveiling of Tristessa as a man:

> *That* was why he had been the perfect man's woman! He had made himself the shrine of his own desires, had made of himself the only woman he could have loved! If a woman is indeed beautiful only in so far as she incarnates most completely the secret aspirations of man,

no wonder Tristessa had been able to become the most beautiful woman in the world, an unbegotten woman who made no concessions to humanity. (128–9)

Woman as the sign made flesh, an unbegotten woman, the product of a man. Carter implicitly contrasts this fabricated woman with two others: Eve, who is made by Mother, and is referred to as a virgin birth, a fully female product; and Mother herself, who, being divinely female and the origin of the principle of femininity, has made herself. Thus, women and men make themselves in each other's image in a sterile binary exchange, and Carter is equally critical of both because she wants to work outside and beyond this unproductive economy of signification. The emphasis is on many selves, on a multiplicity of ways to be, on the fact that reflections do not simply provide mirror-images, but breed new meanings and multiply possibilities (Sage, 1992: 168–77).

The making of women and men and, in particular, the performative nature of gender identity and gender assignment are also continuously signalled throughout the text, and this is done, in part, through the making and remaking of bodies. Carter destabilizes the notion that biological sex is a necessary feature of bodily identity by making sexes fit genders only to show that they do not. Eve, as the sign made flesh, says: 'For, I am not natural you know – even though, if you cut me, I will bleed' (50). All that the sign signifies is false; signs, symbols and representations, however flexible, are always too rigid for the subtleties of living ambiguities. These remain forever uncaptured.

The stuff of the imagination

One does not have to be a great literary critic to hear echoes of Freud, Nietzsche, de Beauvoir and Foucault in Carter's novel. I do not wish to make a reductive argument here, but I would want to argue for a kind of genealogy of the imagination. Carter does not represent the work of these authors, she is not guided by it; rather she plays with metaphors, ways of thinking, ideas about symbols which seem comprehensible because they are already worked in as the stuff of our imaginations, we the readers. We do not have to read in any one particular way; we can be slavish followers of

Carter's playful critique of Freud, or we can be wholly ignorant of it. Our enjoyment is independent of both. And enjoyment is what it is all about. As Carter herself wrote of the political positioning of her work:

> Well, yes; of course. I always hope it's obvious, although I try, when I write fiction, to think on my feet – to present a number of propositions in a variety of different ways, and to leave the reader to construct her own fiction for herself from the elements of my fictions. (Reading is just as creative an activity as writing and most intellectual development depends upon new readings of old texts. I am all for putting new wine in old bottles, especially if the pressure of the new wine makes the old bottles explode.) (1983: 69)

The Passion of New Eve fairly fizzes with the sound of popping corks, and it is, in spite of its potential seriousness, enormously enjoyable. Part of the enjoyment, at least for me, comes from the game of recognition which Carter's fiction demands; the rereading of old texts, except that many of the texts involved are not very old. Carter's fascination with myths, fairy tales and Greek symbolism is certainly there. The symbolically castrated Zero is one-eyed and one-legged. Eve, the virgin birth, is fashioned through the excision of male parts. A whole host of allusions to Christian and classical mythology permeates the text. This would not be of particular interest were it not for the fact that these older symbolic constructions come forward to us in newer form, sometimes refigured as the discoveries of modern intellectual interpretation and scientific practice. To put it at its most obvious, how many of us now when we think of Oedipus, think of the original Greek myth or of Sophocles' play? Few of us, I would tentatively suggest, because our minds run straight away to Freud. Freud's theory of the Oedipus complex is convincing partly because of the metaphoric and symbolic resonances which attach to our comprehension of it, and that is also why it was powerful for Freud himself. What, then, is the status of this theory? What role do the symbolic and the fictive play in the setting up of a model about the so-called real? These are not new thoughts, in fact they are rather old ones, but the general point remains in relation to my discussion of feminism and anthropology. What part do the fictional and the symbolic play in setting up our intellectual models of the world, a world we assume to be real?

In spite of its grotesque and fantastic nature, Carter intends her fiction to have a relation to a lived world outside that fiction. The question is, where does she get her models from? Aside from the sources I have already mentioned, it seems clear to me that she draws on feminist theory and on anthropology. The very distinction between sex and gender, and subsequent theories of the socially constructed and performative nature of gender, came into feminist writing largely from anthropology. In making this statement I do not want to make an origins claim, nor indeed to assert anything about anthropology's contribution to feminism, but rather I want to draw attention to the way in which, via feminism and a number of other routes, anthropology has entered the domain of the popular. Perhaps I should be cautious here and simply say that I think this to be the case for certain registers of the popular in the United Kingdom. The ability to imagine other worlds, alternative forms of sociality, is something which has probably always depended on travellers' accounts, as well as on the mythic, but in our own century it has depended crucially on anthropology (Pratt, 1986, 1992; Thornton, 1983; see chapter 6 of this volume). This means that as Carter works and reworks the relationship between sex and gender, between the feminine and the masculine and actual women and men, she is no more free of anthropology than she is of Freud or Lacan. The grounds for recognizing such things as alternative conceptions of sociality, or a reformulated relationship between bodies and sexual identity, or the utopian matriarchy ruled by Mother, depend on ideas and forms of representation evident in anthropology, as well as in a variety of other contexts and disciplines.

When I say that Carter draws on anthropology, I do not mean to imply that she has been reading Malinowski or poring over kinship diagrams. I simply want to suggest that anthropology, as a way of viewing social relations and, most particularly, relations of otherness, provides one of the imaginative contexts for Carter's work. I focus on anthropology, and on its relation to feminism, because that is what interests me. In fact, part of the fun in reading Carter is that she ranges much more widely than this, and uses narratives and forms of representation based on a variety of disciplines and popular cultural forms, most notably, in the case of *The Passion of New Eve*, the cinema. Consequently, she very often sounds as though she has been reading Teresa de Lauretis or Laura Mulvey.

This may seem like a particularly perverted form of enjoyment, and it is certainly based on a very specific sort of reading – one that would not interest many of Carter's readers, who are involved in deriving their own kinds of enjoyment from the text. However, if I am permitted my own perversions, then there are one or two further points to be made.

I am ultimately less interested perhaps in the origins of Carter's models than I am in the idea that anthropologists and feminists draw their intellectual inspiration from imaginative possibilities that are often worked out for them in fictive contexts. This fact is made even more pertinent by the acknowledgement that games of recognition involve not only elements of self-recognition, but also elements of discursive or disciplinary recognition. The two are connected and quite often it is a matter of recognizing oneself, or an aspect of oneself, in one's disciplinary guise. And, as I have already suggested, this is part of the pleasure for me, as a feminist anthropologist, in reading Angela Carter, as a feminist novelist.

The language of mirrors

One of the most pleasurable things about *The Passion of New Eve* is the way in which Carter handles the relationship between gender identity and language. Carter intimates that gender is always a matter of impersonation, and that we should be constantly aware of the constructed nature of gender identity. This theme is most evident in the actual physical construction of Eve at Mother's hands, but the fundamentally illusory nature of that making is reinforced by the fact that during her convalescence Eve is subjected to a series of rolling images, including endless reruns of old Hollywood movies starring Tristessa. The irony, of course, is that Eve's identification with femininity is achieved by identifying with a man who personifies woman as made in the image of himself. But the irony goes deeper than this, because, as it turns out, Mother has always known that Tristessa is a man. So what are we to make of her choice of Tristessa's femininity as a role model for the newly fashioned Eve? Perhaps the perfect woman does not exist, except as a male construct, a male fantasy.

Carter clearly has larger ideas in mind about the role of the cinema in the social construction of femininity and masculinity, but her more constant theme here is about mirrors and the fantastical nature both of representations and of identifications. When Zero unveils Tristessa as a man and then forces a mock marriage between Eve dressed in men's clothing and Tristessa adorned in a bridal gown, Eve gloomily reflects on the relationship between illusion and identity:

> I had become my old self again in the inverted world of the mirrors. But this masquerade was more than skin deep. Under the mask of maleness I wore another mask of femaleness but a mask that now I never would be able to remove, no matter how hard I tried, although I was a boy disguised as a girl and now disguised as a boy again, like Rosalind in Elizabethan Arden. (132)

The theme of mirrors is a fascinating one and it marks out Carter's preoccupation with the local, partial, illusionary nature of representations of all kinds, whether they be the filmic images of Tristessa's femininity or the day-to-day presentations of gendered selves. Part of Carter's concern with mirrors has to do with the construction of female selves, with woman's identification with herself as object, and with the narcissistic loss of being on which that process depends. It starts with Evelyn's fascinated compulsion for Leilah, the young black woman whom he encounters in New York at the beginning of the novel. Evelyn watches Leilah dressing to go out at night, creating the image of seductive femininity on which her living depends:

> The cracked mirror jaggedly reciprocated her bisected reflection and that of my watching self . . . [she] seemed to abandon herself in the mirror, to abandon herself to the mirror, and allowed herself to function only as a fiction of the erotic dream into which the mirror cast me . . . So, together, we entered the same reverie, the self-created, self-perpetuating, solipsistic world of the woman watching herself being watched in a mirror that seemed to have split apart under the strain of supporting her world. (30)

Femininity is constructed in the male gaze, and identifying with it requires effort; it is a strain. Carter's revenge is appropriately savage, because when Evelyn emerges as Eve, she is revealed to herself as a woman for the first time by her image in the mirror:

> Let the punishment fit the crime, whatever it had been. They had turned me into the *Playboy* centre fold. I was the object of all the unfocused desires that had ever existed in my own head. I had become my own masturbatory fantasy. (75)

The result of this perfect fashioning is a measure of disbelief. Eve's perfection, both physical and behavioural, is achieved through artifice, but at a cost:

> This intensive study of feminine manners . . . kept me in a state of permanent exhaustion . . . although I was a woman, I was now also passing for a woman, but, then many women born spend their whole lives in just such imitations. (101)

Gender is a construct, a masquerade, a performance, a parody. Consequently, the remaking of the body is not enough; the right genitals might be a necessary, but they are not a sufficient condition. What is more, as Eve works at passing as a woman, she arouses suspicion because she is just too perfect, too feminine, too categorically female. Amusingly enough, the artifice is evident not in its failure but in its success. Carter is enjoying herself and she wants us to see the reflection in the mirror, to understand the split nature of identity and to read the doubleness back into gender. Carter often works with the figure of the double in her fiction, but ultimately she wants to subvert this binary economy. It is not sufficient, therefore, to read doubleness back into gender and self-identity, one must go further and see multiplicity. To this end, some of Carter's doubles turn out in the end to be triples, and as such their identity is fashioned outside the constraints of the binary economy. Leilah is one such figure in *The Passion of New Eve*; when we encounter her again towards the end of the novel, she is presented to us as at least three selves (175).

Much of Carter's treatment of mirrors and multiple selves suggests, on occasion, that she is providing us with a ludic feminist rereading of Freud based on Lacan, or perhaps just playing with bits and pieces, various ideas loosely based on the rag-bag of neo-Lacanian ideas that surface and resurface in feminist theorizing. This suggestion could appear either reductionist or far-fetched, depending on how you choose to look at it. But my contention is that Carter enjoys this kind of game, and she encourages her readers to derive pleasure from games of recognition based on their knowledge of psychoanalytic and feminist theory. Such knowledge is not a prerequisite for understanding or enjoying the novel. Carter would never be either so concrete or so intellectually vulgar; she, after all, is playing her own games with her self(ves).

In Lacanian theory the mirror stage marks the inauguration of recognition and its association with pleasure. As the child gradually comes to understand that the reflection is an image of itself, it becomes enamoured of its specular double, and begins to take up an exterior perspective on itself, so that ultimately it will be capable of representing itself to itself. However, the Lacanian subject is a divided one, because its identity is premised on an image of itself which is not itself; in other words, it is based on the recognition of its mirror-image as its self-as-other. The mirror stage divides the subject 'between a body it claims as its own and an other it strives to be like' (Grosz, 1990: 42). But the Imaginary order inaugurated by the mirror stage does not allow the child to act as an agent or subject within the world. While the child remains bound to its double, it cannot engage in social relations with others; for this to be possible, the child must enter the Symbolic order.

Entry into the Symbolic provides the conditions for social, linguistic and economic exchange, and this involves being positioned in relation to the law of the father. The phallus is the privileged signifier of the Symbolic order, and the relations each sex has to the signifier determine their positions as feminine or masculine subjects within the patriarchal Symbolic order. There is much debate about Lacan's phallocentrism (see chapter 2), but what is clear is that the penis does become elided with the phallus and functions as an imaginary object dividing the sexes, according to its presence or absence, thus acting as a symbolic object of relations between them. The important point about the phallus, however, is that as the signifier of signifiers it represents language, and it is by means of a relation to this signifier that the subject comes to occupy the position of the 'I' in discourse, and acquires a speaking position. Since both sexes are constructed as sexually different with reference to the phallic signifier, the feminine and the masculine, for Lacan, are a function of language.

Carter plays with the relationship between language and sexed identities in very interesting ways. At the beginning of the novel Evelyn constantly represents Leilah's mystique and her sexual allure for him as connected to her otherness and to her less than human status; and he does so by commenting on her lack of comprehensibility, her lack of language.

> Her argot or patois was infinitely strange to me, I could hardly understand a word she said but I was mad for her . . . (26)

> Sometimes, when I was exhausted and she was not . . . she would clamber on top of me in the middle of the night . . . and thrust my limp cock inside herself, twittering away as she did so like a distracted canary. (27)

Desire is an effect of language, or rather a lack of it. Sexual difference is certainly a matter of language, where having or not having the penis is symbolically equated with having or not having language. Carter pursues the link between feminine identity and the possession of language in later sections of the book where she describes Zero's harem and the world he forces upon those he has captured. Zero forbids his seven wives to speak in words, and so in his presence they speak in babble and gibberish, although they can all talk perfectly well. Zero himself talks to his wives only 'in the language of animals', in barks, grunts and squeaks, and he forces them to answer him in kind.

> So our first words every morning were spoken in a language we ourselves could not understand; but he could. Or so he claimed, and, because he ruled the roost and his word was law, it came to the same thing. So he regulated our understanding of him and also our understanding of ourselves in relation to him. (96–7)

Zero, then, embodies the principle of the law of the father – he controls language. More than this, he controls the world he and his wives inhabit both by imposing an arbitrary order of social relations and by restricting contact with the real world. He forbids newspapers and any access to independent accounts or representations of the world outside the world he has constructed. 'He no longer needed news of the world, since he manufactured it himself to his own designs' (101). The only forms of representation he permits are strange cabaret acts performed to the music of Wagner in which he constantly re-enacts his future imagined triumph over Tristessa, whom he blames for his impotence.

Zero not only lays down the form of language and the conditions for linguistic exchange, but he also imposes arbitrary sets of social relations. Zero ranks pigs and dogs above women, and orders social hierarchies accordingly. He also denies his wives any cutlery, meat, soap or shoes, any of the 'paraphernalia of modern society'. This, like the denial of their linguistic competence, marks out their pre-cultural, non-male status.

Carter, however, never preaches and no single depiction is ever allowed to stand unchallenged. Zero is a poor representative of the omnipotent symbolic Father. He is, after all, one-eyed and one-legged, symbolically castrated and literally memberless. His impotence is the source of his murderous desire for revenge, and his attempts to control the world through controlling the grounds for signification are simply attempts to cover over his lack. Carter enjoys herself here and makes sure that we understand that while Zero is happy to display his private parts, he is paralysingly coy about his amputated stump, which he never uncovers or allows any of his wives to see. The real evidence for Zero's inadequacies as a patriarch, his inability to successfully inaugurate culture, is his own relation to language. He is a poet, but he no longer writes down his poetry, he bays it out over the desert, expressing himself in dance, expletives and *tableaux vivants*. He eschews everyday human speech, except in circumstances of dire necessity, preferring barks and grunts. He cannot control language or the world he has created, and thus he is truly impotent.

In many ways Zero's antithesis is Mother. Once human, she has made herself divine: 'She is the hand-carved figurehead of her own, self-constructed theology' (58). Mother has to retire from the God-head at the end of the novel because she realizes that she has failed in her attempt to control time, history and symbolism! None the less, Mother is constantly represented as 'a figure of speech', 'a sign made flesh'. It is Mother, not Zero, who embodies language, but still the living world remains outside the control even of her Law.

Lacan argues, of course, that both sexes are constituted as sexually differentiated only with reference to the phallic signifier, but as the signifier of differences, the phallus is also the term which functions to bring the sexes together, and acts as a symbol of their union. For both sexes, albeit in different ways, the phallus functions as the means of access to the domain of the Other, understood here as the socio-symbolic network. Since the Other, organized around the phallus as primary signifier, is the condition of sexual difference, one can only seek one's other (woman or man) through the Other. One must assume here, as Lacan does, that the phallus is an object of desire, but without the mediation of the other and the Other, no one can have access to it. It is in the 'comedy of copulation' that each affirms their relation to the phallus and to the socio-symbolic order, and as such the phallus functions as symbolic mediator between the sexes, both uniting them and dividing them (Lacan, 1977: 289). Sexual relations, then, are bound up with a circuit of exchange.

It is Tristessa who personifies this circuit in the novel, as well as its breakdown. When Eve sees that Tristessa is a man, she says:

> and when I saw how much the heraldic regalia of his sex appalled him, I thought that Mother would say he had become a woman because he had abhorred his most female part – that is, his instrument of mediation between himself and the other. (128)

This piece of clarified thought only makes sense to us later on in the novel when we come to understand that Mother has always known that Tristessa was a man because many years before he had approached her asking for a sex-change operation. Mother refused him:

> Mama told me, he was too much of a woman, already, for the good of the sex; and besides, when she subjected him to the first tests, she was struck by what seemed to her the awfully ineradicable quality of his maleness. (173)

Too feminine for the good of the sex because she was, of course, woman created in man's image. But what of the ineradicable maleness? This too is explained to Eve:

> Abandoned on this great continent like a star in space, an atomised, fragmented existence, his cock stuck in his asshole so that he himself formed the uroborus, the perfect circle, the vicious circle, the dead end. (173)

Ineradicably male because he abhorred his feminine part; he refused to mediate with the other, to enter the circle of exchange. Outside the Symbolic order he is a self without a self, a fragment lost in a void. He inhabits a space without signification.

The contexts of the imagination

It is not difficult to suggest, then, that in *The Passion of New Eve* Angela Carter plays with much that she has inherited from feminism, psychoanalysis and anthropology and, since these discourses all intertwine to a certain degree, it is not possible or necessary to be clear about the causal or evolutionary sequence of influences. However, as a feminist anthropologist engaged in dialogue with persons who have very different ideas about gender from my own, I have to wonder about the origins of my models, the nature of the influences working upon me, the stuff of my imagination. I do not have a definitive answer to this question, but I do know that straightforwardly anthropological writing informs my imagination relatively little. It certainly provides me with a set of co-ordinates, a series of arguments to debate with, a set of comparative materials and a number of imagined entities. What I am aware of – most often when I lecture on gender issues, rather than when I am actually writing – is that communication between colleagues, both feminists and anthropologists, is a fragile business. I used to say, not a little tongue-in-cheek, that one of the problems with lecturing on gender is that everybody thinks they know all about it before you open your mouth because they have already got one – a gender, that is. This gender is, of course, one that is based on experience, but it is also one that is heavily symbolized. Through our engagement in an intersubjective world, we invest our bodily experiences with the power of symbols, and thus we arrive at a certain (mis)understanding of both. No wonder, then, that audiences sometimes resist when you try to tell them a story about gender which, whilst masquerading as an intellectual model, is thoroughly redolent of one's own narrative of understanding.

My intellectual models, including my readings of Freud, Lacan, Angela Carter and feminist and anthropological theory in general, have been profoundly altered through dialogue with the people I have worked with, those who have had the misfortune to be the subjects of my anthropological enquiries. Their views of gender, and of social and sexual relations, are now part of the general paraphernalia I bring to bear when thinking about pretty much anything, including how to read Angela Carter's novels. However, I am more concerned with how the process works the other way round, with how anthropologists interpret alternative gender models and gender systems in terms of a set of intellectual models drawn from psychoanalysis, anthropology, feminism and other sources which purport to be general theories when they are little more than local folk models. One way in which we can acknowledge that the academic is often the popular in disguise is to use alternative ways of thinking about categories, concepts and processes to critique our local models, to destabilize them and force us to expand our horizons. Anthropologists often claim they do this by going to study 'other cultures', and this may be the case. But one of the major ways we do this is through engagement with fictions and fictive representations, through reading about or viewing reinterpretations of gender categories, symbols and processes. The popular in many forms – and I have only discussed one such form – provides the imaginative impetus for academic models and discourses of all kinds. I am aware that this could sound like that ancient chestnut, once so popular in critical circles, about the expansion of one's human understanding through the medium of Art (capital A)! I have nothing so grand in mind. I am simply saying that one of the ways in which we learn about, for example, the possibility of a sexual economy that is unrestricted by the sterility of binary exchange is to read a fictive account of such a possibility. Fictional narratives may themselves be informed by versions of academic models, as I have suggested for *The Passion of New Eve*, but these fictions will, in their turn, inform future academic theories. Intellectual models depend for their impetus on imaginative possibilities they themselves cannot provide. What masquerades as the academic is very often the popular

in disguise, and we would do well to remember that this sophisticated veiling mechanism is merely one of the more commonplace methods for covering over what we do not wish to have
revealed.

NOTES

Introduction   A Passion for Difference

1 Michèlle Barrett (1987) has discussed some of the ways in which the term is habitually employed.

Chapter 1   The Divisions Within:
Sex, Gender and Sexual Difference

1 This paper was orginally presented at a conference on feminist theory at the University of Essex in February 1993. My inspiration for publishing the piece in this form comes from my reading of Nancy Miller's attempt to explicate the politics and contingencies of identity and location (1991). I am also grateful for Marianna Torgovnick's discussion of the use of the pronoun 'we' (1990: 4).
2 One such concept was the family: Amos and Parmar, 1984; Bhavnani and Colson, 1986; Collins, 1989, 1990.
3 The literature is very extensive, but for examples from history, anthropology and literature see Epstein and Straub, 1991; W. Williams, 1986; and Garber, 1992.
4 Lévi-Strauss (1969) first identified the flesh–bone complex. See, for example, Diemberger, 1993, and for further discussion Moore, 1993a.
5 Again, the literature is large, but for examples see Sanday and Goodenough, 1990, and Atkinson and Errington, 1990.
6 Catherine MacKinnon, 'Women and Human Rights', Amnesty Lecture, Oxford, 5 February 1993.

7 Most notable in this regard is the work of French feminists, particularly Kristeva (1980) and Cixous (1981, 1986); although Anglo-American scholars are also involved in this move, they proceed from different premises, and criticisms of the French school abound. See, for example, Suleiman, 1986; Gallop, 1988; Burke, 1980; Rich, 1976; Conley, 1984; Stanton, 1986; Spivak, 1992; Silverman, 1988; Delphy, 1975; and Grosz, 1989.

8 Butler (1990: ch. 3) argues that Foucault's position provides for a critique of Lacanian and neo-Lacanian theories. On this basis, she criticizes Kristeva's view of the maternal body as pre-symbolic, but without apparently recognizing the perils of her own neo-Foucauldian position.

9 Braidotti refuses to confront this issue, and effectively claims that gender and sexual difference are the same thing and/or that the difference between them is not significant (1991: 264).

Chapter 2 Embodied Selves: Dialogues between Anthropology and Psychoanalysis

1 The only notable exception in this regard are recent studies in that area of ethnopsychology that has become known as the 'anthropology of emotion': see Abu-Lughod, 1986; Lutz, 1988; and Lutz and Abu-Lughod, 1990.

2 A great deal of new research from Melanesia does deal with problems of identity and sexual difference for males: see Herdt, 1982, 1984, and Herdt and Stoler, 1990.

3 The literature in this field is vast, but for recent overviews that provide a sense of the history of the field's development and the range of debates involved, as well as useful references, see Shweder, 1991: chs 3 and 4, and Whittaker, 1992.

4 For a recent and very helpful contribution see Mahoney and Yngvesson, 1992.

5 McHugh (1989) has recently made this point using data on the Gurungs of Nepal and contra Dumont and Marriott. Gewertz (1984) has also recently criticized Margaret Mead and Nancy Chodorow (who uses Mead's original material) for assessing the strength and weaknesses of Tchambuli women in terms of their ability to individuate or act as individuals. Gewertz's argument is simply that such an approach is ethnocentric.

6 I am greatly indebted to Judith Butler. Her work on gender identity has provided the inspiration for my argument in this section (Butler, 1990).

7 See Roland, 1988, for a brilliant case study that challenges the universal nature of psychoanalytic theory and demonstrates how ethnocentric many of its assumptions are.

8 This is most particularly the case given that for Lacan, the recognition of different sexed subject positions, consequent on the threat of castration, depends on the fact that each sex confuses the phallic signifier with a part or whole of its body. There is absolutely no reason why we should assume that this process of symbolic substitution and condensation is a universal one, or rather that as a process it proceeds in a universal manner.

9 I take Bourdieu to be making a parallel point when he criticizes Lacan's account of the significance of the phallus (Bourdieu, 1990a: 4, 14) and points out that what psychoanalysts rediscover in the functioning of the unconscious are the unthought categories of their own thought. Bourdieu stops short of characterizing psychoanalysis as ethnocentric, but what he does say is: 'Il faudrait évidemment pousser beaucoup plus loin la lecture *anthropologique* des textes psychanalytiques, de leurs présupposés, de leurs sousentendus et de leurs lapsus' (1990a: 4). The fact that psychoanalysis encodes Eurocentric ideas about gender, that what psychoanalysts use to think gender are their own ideas about gender, should not surprise us.

Chapter 3   Fantasies of Power and Fantasies of Identity: Gender, Race and Violence

1 Michel Foucault's work is foremost in this regard (1977, 1978, 1985, 1986). Summaries and critiques of Foucault's work abound, but for an excellent reappraisal from a feminist perspective and a full treatment of his later works see McNay, 1992.

2 This is a point that anthropologists have been slow to take up, but see Sacks, 1989. Women of colour theorists argued from an early date that race and gender were experienced simultaneously and could not be separated into discrete analytic categories (Davis, 1981; hooks, 1984). Recent work on women in the workplace in the United States provides ample evidence that women workers themselves recognize the mutually constitutive nature of gender and race; for overviews see Collins, 1990: ch. 3, and Glenn, 1992.

3 A notable exception in this regard was the work of Obeyesekere (1981). Much recent research in psychoanalytic and psychological anthropology has also provided a critique of these older assumptions (see chapter 2).

4   Recent critiques in anthropology have questioned whether a notion of 'society' can stand as a pre-given around which we can orient our work (e.g. Strathern, 1988), but the notion of the individual as singular and as maintaining an unproblematic relationship to a material entity has remained pretty well untouched.

5   For an overview of various post-structuralist positions on the subject and subjectivity see P. Smith, 1988.

6   The intersections of race and gender in the context of colonialism and imperialism have been addressed by many scholars and the literature is large, but see Stoler, 1989; 1991, for informative argument and overviews.

7   'One change in direction that would be real cool would be the production of a discourse on race that interrogates whiteness . . . In far too much contemporary writing . . . race is always an issue of Otherness that is not white; it is black, brown, yellow, red, purple even' (hooks, 1991: 54); see also Collins, 1990. Toni Morrison (1992) discusses the unmarked nature of the category 'white' in the American literary tradition.

8   For excellent discussions of the way the discourses of race and otherness have changed over time see Vaughan, 1991, and Thomas, 1994. Both these scholars point out how discourses of racial otherness are crucial for the construction of white identity.

9   Feminist scholars were the first to make arguments of this kind, but more recently this theme has emerged in the writing of those concerned with men's studies and with theorizing masculinity. Connell's very clear theoretical statement (1987) is clearly derived from his reading of feminist texts.

Chapter 4   Bodies on the Move: Gender, Power and Material Culture

1   In anthropology this has much to do with the downgrading of the study of material culture, although it is now enjoying something of a renaissance (see Moore, 1986). Architects, geographers and archaeologists have not been so neglectful of these matters. See, for example, Soja, 1989; Gregory and Urry, 1985; Pred, 1990; Hodder, 1991; and Tilley, 1990.

2   Denise Riley (1988) discusses the difficult relationship women qua women have to the category 'woman', and how that relationship has changed over time.

3   I believe that actors can bring such principles to discourse precisely because praxis can act as a moment of critical reflection. The situations

and circumstances under which this becomes possible would have to be specified analytically and descriptively. Bourdieu, however, normally emphasizes that such principles are rarely brought to discourse, though he believes it is possible through an external process of clarification – a kind of consciousness raising. He also emphasizes, of course, and most notably with regard to gender, that the heritage of Descartes in the social sciences has meant that analysts are happy to discuss the agent's self-reflexive abilities, their reflections on action, but less willing to see action itself as a type of critical reflection (1990a: 12).

4 See Bourdieu and Wacquant, 1992: 79–83, for a list of these critics and for a response from Bourdieu.

5 Bourdieu has produced a mass of empirical sociology, and as such his work is full of examples, but few of them can be used to demonstrate processes of social change.

6 One of Bourdieu's chief criticisms is that psychoanalysis reduces the relation to the body to the sexual (1990c: 77). However, Bourdieu does acknowledge the importance of fantasy, desire and self-image in his discussion of gender differences and masculine domination (1990a). Bourdieu is critical of psychoanalysis in this paper, but he also approaches it more positively than elsewhere, partly because he is concerned to link the body and body praxis to notions of identity and, in particular, to sexed identities.

7 This produces a strange and unresolved tension where Bourdieu gives undue weight to childhood experiences, and indeed family interactions, but does not wish to integrate a psychoanalytic approach into his work.

8 Bourdieu has said that he wants to escape from the philosophy of the subject without doing away with the agent (1985). This seems to be connected with Bourdieu's estrangement from French psychoanalysis, and he has certainly not attempted to develop a theory of subjectivity, but, once again, it is significant that he comes closest to having to treat this problem in his discussion of the nature of gender differences and masculine domination (1990a).

9 Bourdieu does make a number of very important assertions about female subjectivity, without actually using the term 'subjectivity', in his essay on masculine domination (1990a: 26–9). One is that women are not able to be subjects in the same way as men, since subjectivity is defined in the male mode, so to speak. However, Bourdieu links this difference not only to women's position within relations of production and reproduction, but to their relationship to the acquisition of symbolic capital (1990a: 28).

10 Bourdieu is well aware that other forms of difference are important as well as those of gender and class (1990b: ch. 8, 1990a). However, he has

made little attempt to theorize these axes of differentiation in terms of the concept of habitus. What Bourdieu's theory lacks is a notion of the multiplicity and simultaneity of difference.

11 The work of Chicana scholars has been notable in this regard, especially their treatment of narrative and personal history. see, for example, Anzaldúa, 1987, and articles by Sommer, 1988, and Alarcon, 1990, for a discussion of these issues.

12 This is exactly the point made by James Scott (1985) in his analysis of forms of peasant resistance, but from a rather different perspective. Bourdieu also emphasizes that actions can supply moments of reinterpretation and reformulation that have the potential to provide the conditions for resistance. However, he stresses that in the case of women and masculine domination all forms of resistance take place within the symbolic categories of the dominant male world view, and that symbolic revolution would have to be a collective act (1990a: 15, 30). Bourdieu certainly believes resistance is possible (see his analysis of resistance by Algerian peasants to the imposition of colonialism, 1979), but he sees it as being the product of collective rather than individual action, and he is critical of what he calls spontaneous populism because of his view that the dominated rarely escape the power relations of the dominated/dominant divide (1991: 90–102).

13 Bourdieu makes this point also about the habitus, and this is why he believes that his theory incorporates the potential for social change (1990a: 15, 1990c).

14 I draw all my examples in this section from the work of Dolores Hayden (1981), and I base my discussion of these issues on her material and on the work of Barbara Taylor (1983). The gender politics of these nineteenth-century feminist reformers were notably radical, but their race and class politics generally not.

Chapter 5   Social Identities and the Politics of Reproduction

1 Some feminist-Marxist writing on the household treats it as a unit that jointly chooses to deploy its labour power to maximize the interests of all its members. This view is particularly prevalent in work that stresses family strategies, adaptations and choices, as though the family/household were an undifferentiated unit (e.g. Humphries, 1979; Arizpe, 1982).

2 An examination of recent research findings suggests that it is far from clear that inequalities within the household can be systematically related to the economic bargaining power of household members.

Hartmann concluded on the basis of her work in the USA that women are not able to translate their wages into reduced work weeks or labour substitution (1981: 381). Hoodfar argues that while some researchers have indicated that a wife's power relative to her husband's increases when she is a wage earner, her own data from Cairo suggests that power of wives can decrease once they are earning wages that are subsequently designated as being for collective family needs (1988: 134–5). A number of feminist scholars have argued that women have little knowledge of how much their husband's earn and of what their assets are (Pahl, 1989; Hoodfar, 1988; Fapohunda, 1988; Roldan, 1988). This point is important because it emphasizes that control over and access to knowledge about household resources is often as important as control over decision-making. Thus, women and men begin the process of bargaining from very different starting points. For fuller discussion of these points see Moore, 1993b.

3 This is also the problem with Meillassoux's work on reproduction, because in spite of his discussion of marriage strategies and agricultural resources, he basically assumes that as long as households reproduce society will be reproduced (1981).

4 My analytical and theoretical approach in this essay has been strongly influenced by the work of Joan Acker (1988), from whom I took the term 'system of distribution' and turned it into the slightly different concept of the 'system of redistribution'.

Chapter 6   Master Narratives: Anthropology and Writing

1 For excellent feminist reviews of these issues see Mascia-Lees, Sharpe and Cohen, 1989; 1991; Abu-Lughod, 1991; and Kirby, 1989; 1991.

2 My arguments about anthropology and its similarities with other forms of writing, especially travel writing, are indebted to Mary Louise Pratt, on whose work I have drawn extensively for inspiration at a number of points in this text; see in particular Pratt, 1986; 1992: 30, ch. 9. Pratt makes the point that from the eighteenth century onwards European knowledge of natural history, landscape and other cultures was constructed through the mediation of printed texts.

3 Pratt (1992: ch. 9) argues that individuals like Henry Stanley, Roger Casement and Joseph Conrad, and subsequently Albert Camus and Richard Wright, were hyphenated white men armed with pens; and that their own hyphenated or split origins and identities gave them some special advantage when it came to representing 'contact situations', a kind of double perspective that served as a form of critique.

4   Elspeth Probyn makes the same point (1993: ch. 3).
5   The feminist theorizing of the notion of subject position and positionality often proceeds without any reference to the Althusserian concept of interpellation, in spite of the fact that there are obvious continuities. For further illuminating discussion of the notion of subject positions and their relationship to discourses see Weedon, 1987, and P. Smith, 1988; see also chapter 3 of this volume.
6   This point has been made by Clifford (1988: ch. 1) and others, but Mary Louise Pratt has pointed out how the collective 'they' elides easily in travel writing with the iconic 'he' (1992: 64), and I find her analysis very pertinent here.
7   Lutz has recently discussed the way in which women's writing gets erased in anthropology (1990).
8   Kirby makes a similar point about the 'new anthropologist' and the 'new ethnography' (1993: 130).

Chapter 7   The Feminist Anthropologist and the Passion(s) of New Eve

1   For critiques on this point see Clifford's rereading of Said, 1988, and Ahmad, 1992. Paradoxically, cultural studies and colonial discourse theory are complicit in this process because in criticizing the material and discursive domination, exploitation and expropriation of the West, both now and in the past, they provide the conditions for its continuing reification as a category with powerful ideological effects. Thus, their discourse is no more free of the familiar 'us'/'them' dichotomies than is anthropology, and they continually reinscribe the relations of 'otherness' they seek to transcend.
2   The most blatant and disturbing example of this recently in the UK has been the debate about whether homosexuality is genetically determined.
3   Of this particular novel Carter wrote: 'I conceived it as a feminist tract about the social creation of femininity, amongst other things' (1983: 71).
4   It seems to me that much British anthropological writing implicitly uses the realist novel as its model, but this is never discussed. Austen and Trollope spring to mind.
5   British anthropology is another fictional category, like that of the West. I do not, therefore, use the term 'British context' to imply persons living and working in the UK. Once again, it is a matter of positionalities and of discursive effects.

REFERENCES

Abu-Lughod, Lila 1986: *Veiled Sentiments: Honor and Poetry in a Bedouin Society*. Berkeley: University of California Press.

Abu-Lughod, Lila 1991: 'Writing against culture'. In Richard Fox (ed.), *Recapturing Anthropology: Working in the Present*, Santa Fe, N. Mex.: School of American Research.

Acker, Joan 1988: 'Class; gender and the relations of distribution'. *Signs*, 13 (3): 474–97.

Ahmad, Aijat 1992: *In Theory: Classes, Nations, Literatures*. London: Verso.

Alarcon, Norma 1990: 'The theoretical subject(s) of *This Bridge Called My Back* and Anglo-American feminism'. In Gloria Anzaldúa (ed.), *Making Face, Making Soul: Haciendo Caras*, San Francisco: Aunt Lute, 356–69.

Amos, Valerie and Parmar, Pratibha 1984: 'Challenging imperial feminism'. *Feminist Review*, 17: 3–19.

Anzaldúa, Gloria 1987: *Borderlands/La Frontera*. San Francisco: Spinsters/Aunt Lute.

Arizpe, Lourdes 1982: 'Relay migration and the survival of the peasant household'. In Helen Safa (ed.), *Towards a Political Economy of Urbanisation in Third World Countries*, Delhi: Oxford University Press, 19–46.

Atkinson, Jane 1990: 'How gender makes a difference in Wana society'. In Jane Atkinson and Shelly Errington (eds), *Power and Difference: Gender in Island Southeast Asia*, Stanford: Stanford University Press.

Atkinson, Jane and Errington, Shelly (eds) 1990: *Power and Difference: Gender in Island Southeast Asia*. Stanford: Stanford University Press.

Barrett, Michèlle 1980: *Women's Oppression Today*. London: Verso.

Barrett, Michèlle 1987: 'The concept of difference'. *Feminist Review*, 26: 29–41.

Becker, Gary 1976: *The Economic Approach to Human Behavior*. Chicago: University of Chicago Press.

Becker, Gary 1981: *Treatise on the Family*. Cambridge, Mass.: Harvard University Press.

Bell, Amelia Rector 1990: 'Separate people: speaking of Creek men and women'. *American Anthropologist*, 92: 332–45.

Bhavnani, Kum-Kum and Colson, Margaret 1986: 'Transforming socialist-feminism: the challenge of racism'. *Feminist Review*, 23: 81–92.

Bourdieu, Pierre 1977: *Outline of a Theory of Practice*. Cambridge: Cambridge University Press.

Bourdieu, Pierre 1979: *Algeria 1960*. Cambridge: Cambridge University Press.

Bourdieu, Pierre 1985: 'The genesis of the concepts of "habitus" and "field"'. *Sociocriticism*, 2 (2): 11–24.

Bourdieu, Pierre 1988: 'Vive la crise! For heterodoxy in social science'. *Theory and Society*, 17 (5): 773–88.

Bourdieu, Pierre 1990a: 'La Domination masculine'. *Actes de la recherche en sciences sociales*, 84: 2–31.

Bourdieu, Pierre 1990b: *In Other Words*. Cambridge: Polity Press.

Bourdieu, Pierre 1990c: *The Logic of Practice*. Cambridge: Polity Press.

Bourdieu, Pierre 1991: *Language and Symbolic Power*. Cambridge: Polity Press.

Bourdieu, Pierre and Wacquant, Loic 1992: *An Invitation to Reflexive Sociology*. Cambridge: Polity Press.

Braidotti, Rosi 1991: *Patterns of Dissonance*. Cambridge: Polity Press.

Brennan, Teresa (ed.) 1989: *Between Feminism and Psychoanalysis*. London: Routledge.

Burke, Carolyn 1980: 'Rethinking the maternal'. In Hester Eisenstein and Alice Jardine (eds), *The Future of Difference*, New York: Barnard College Women's Center.

Butler, Judith 1990: *Gender Trouble: Feminism and the Subversion of Identity*. London: Routledge.

Carney, Judith and Watts, Michael 1990: 'Manufacturing dissent: work, gender and the politics of meaning in a peasant society'. *Africa*, 60: 207–41.

Carter, Angela 1983: 'Notes from the front line'. In Michelene Wandor (ed.), *On Gender and Writing*, London: Pandora Press, 69–77.

Cixous, Hélène 1981: 'The laugh of the Medusa'. In Elaine Marks and Isabelle de Courtivron (eds), *New French Feminisms*, London: Harvester Press, 245–64.

Cixous, Hélène 1986: *Entre l'écriture*. Paris: des femmes.

Clifford, James 1986: 'Partial truths'. In James Clifford and George Marcus (eds), *Writing Culture: The Poetics and Politics of Ethnography*, Berkeley: University of California Press, 1–26.

Clifford, James 1988: *The Predicament of Culture*. Cambridge, Mass.: Harvard University Press.

Clifford, James and Marcus, George (eds) 1986: *Writing Culture: The Poetics and Politics of Ethnography*. Berkeley: University of California Press.

Collins, Patricia Hill 1989: 'A comparison of two works on black family life'. *Signs*, 14 (4): 875–84.

Collins, Patricia Hill 1990: *Black Feminist Thought*. London: Unwin Hyman.

Conley, Verena Andermatt 1984: *Hélène Cixous: Writing the Feminine*. Lincoln, Nebr.: University of Nebraska.

Connell, Robert 1987: *Gender and Power*. Cambridge: Polity Press.

Crapanzano, Vincent 1980: *Tuhami: Portrait of a Moroccan*. Chicago: University of Chicago Press.

Crapanzano, Vincent 1992: *Hermes' Dilemma and Hamlet's Desire: Essays in the Epistemology of Interpretation*. Cambridge, Mass.: Harvard University Press.

Davis, Angela 1981: *Women, Race and Class*. New York: Random House.

De Lauretis, Teresa 1984: *Alice Doesn't: Feminism, Semiotics, Cinema*. London: Macmillan.

De Lauretis, Teresa (ed.) 1986: *Feminist Studies/Critical Studies*. London: Macmillan.

De Lauretis, Teresa 1987: *Technologies of Gender: Essays on Theory, Film and Fiction*. London: Macmillan.

Delphy, Christine 1975: 'Proto-feminisme et anti-feminisme'. *Les temps modernes*, 346: 1469–500.

Diemberger, Hildegard 1993: 'Blood, sperm, soul and the mountain: gender relations, kinship and cosmovision among the Khumbo (NE Nepal)'. In Teresa del Valle (ed.), *Gendered Anthropology*, London: Routledge, 88–127.

Dieterlen, Germaine 1941: *Les Âmes des Dogon*. Paris: Institut d'Ethnologie (Travaux et mémoires, 40).

Dumont, Louis 1986: *Essays on Individualism*. Chicago: University of Chicago Press.

Ellen, Roy (ed.) 1981: *Field Research*. London: Academic Press.

Engels, Friedrich [1884] 1972: *The Origin of the Family, Private Property and the State*. New York: Pathfinder Press.

Epstein, Julia and Straub, Kristina 1991: *Body Guards*. London: Routledge.

Evans-Pritchard, Edward [1940] 1969: *The Nuer: A Description of the Modes of the Livelihood and Political Institutions of a Nilotic People*. Oxford: Clarendon Press.

Fapohunda, E. 1978: 'Characteristics of women workers in Lagos'. *Labour and Society*, 3 (2): 258–71.

Fapohunda, E. 1988: 'The non-pooling household: a challenge to theory'. In Daisy Dwyer and Judith Bruce (eds), *A Home Divided*, Stanford: Stanford University Press, 143–54.

Firth, Raymond [1936] 1957: *We, the Tikopia: A Sociological Study of Kinship in Primitive Polynesia*. London: Allen and Unwin.

Flax, Jane 1987: 'Postmodernism and gender relations in feminist theory'. *Signs*, 12 (4): 621–43.

Folbre, Nancy 1984: 'The feminisation of poverty and the pauperisation of motherhood'. *Review of Radical Political Economics*, 16 (4): 78–88.

Folbre, Nancy 1988: 'The black four of hearts: toward a new paradigm of household economics'. In Daisy Dwyer and Judith Bruce (eds), *A Home Divided*, Stanford: Stanford University Press, 248–64.

Fortes, Meyer 1973: 'On the concept of the person among the Tallensi'. In Germaine Dieterlen (ed.), *Colloque international sur le notion de personne en Afrique*, Paris: CRNS, 126–47.

Foucault, Michel 1977: *Discipline and Punish*. Harmondsworth: Peregrine.

Foucault, Michel 1978: *The History of Sexuality*, vol. i. Harmondsworth: Penguin.

Foucault, Michel 1985: *The Use of Pleasure*. Harmondsworth: Penguin.

Foucault, Michel 1986: *The Care of the Self*. Harmondsworth: Penguin.

Fraser, Nancy 1989: *Unruly Practices: Power, Discourse and Gender in Contemporary Social Theory*. Cambridge: Polity Press.

Fuss, Diana 1989: *Essentially Speaking*. London: Routledge.

Gallop, Jane 1982: *Feminism and Psychoanalysis: The Daughter's Seduction*. London: Macmillan.

Gallop, Jane 1988: *Thinking through the Body*. New York: Columbia University Press.

Garber, Marjorie 1992: *Vested Interests*. London: Routledge.

Geertz, Clifford 1988: *Works and Lives: The Anthropologist as Author*. Cambridge: Polity Press.

Gewertz, Deborah 1984: 'The Tchambuli view of persons: a critique of individualism in the works of Mead and Chodorow'. *American Anthropologist*, 86: 615–29.

Giddens, Anthony 1979: *Central Problems in Social Theory*. London: Macmillan.

Giddens, Anthony 1984: *The Constitution of Society*. Cambridge: Polity Press.

Gilman, Charlotte Perkins [1898] 1966: *Women and Economics*. New York: Harper and Row.

Glenn, E. Nakano 1992: 'From servitude to service work: historical continuities in the racial division of paid reproductive labour'. *Signs*, 18 (1): 1–43.

Gregory, David and Urry, John (eds) 1985: *Social Relations and Spatial Structures*. London: Macmillan.

Grosz, Elizabeth 1989: *Sexual Subversions*. London: Allen and Unwin.

Grosz, Elizabeth 1990: *Jacques Lacan: A Feminist Introduction*. London: Routledge.

Guyer, Jane and Peters, Pauline 1987: Introduction. 'Conceptualising the Household'. *Development and Change*, 18: 197–214 [special issue].

Hallowell, A. I. 1971: *Culture and Experience*. New York: Schocken Books.

Harding, Sandra (ed.) 1987: *Feminism and Methodology*. Bloomington: Indiana University Press.

Harris, Olivia 1981: 'Households as natural units'. In Kate Young, Carol Wolkowitz and Roslyn McCullagh (eds), *Of Marriage and the Market*, London: CSE Books, 49–68.

Harris, Olivia and Young, Kate 1981: 'Engendered structures: some problems in the analysis of reproduction'. In Joel Kahn and Josep Llobera (eds), *The Anthropology of Pre-capitalist Societies*, London: Macmillan, 109–47.

Hart, Gillian 1993: 'Imagined unities: constructions of "The household" in economic theory'. In Sutti Ortiz and Susan Lees (eds), *Understanding Economic Process*, Lanham: University Press of America, 111–29.

Hartmann, Heidi 1981: 'The family as the locus of gender, class and political struggle: the example of housework'. *Signs*, 6 (3): 366–94.

Harvey, Penelope 1994: 'Domestic Violence in the Peruvian Andes' In Peter Gow and Penelope Harvey (eds) *Sex and Violence: Issues in Representation and Experience*. London: Routledge.

Hayden, Dolores 1981: *The Grand Domestic Revolution: A History of Feminist Designs for American Homes, Neighborhoods and Cities*. Cambridge, Mass.: Massachusetts Institute of Technology.

Heelas, Paul and Lock, Andrew (eds) 1981: *Indigenous Psychologies: The Anthropology of the Self*. London: Academic Press.

Herdt, Gilbert (ed.) 1982: *Rituals of Manhood: Male Initiation in New Guinea*. Berkeley: University of California Press.

Herdt, Gilbert (ed.) 1984: *Ritualised Homosexuality in Melanesia*. Berkeley: University of California Press.

Herdt, Gilbert and Stoler, Robert 1990: *Intimate Communications: Erotics and the Study of Culture*. New York: Columbia University Press.

Hodder, Ian 1991: *Reading the Past*. Cambridge: Cambridge University Press.

Holloway, Wendy 1984: 'Gender difference and the production of subjectivity'. In Julian Henriques, Wendy Holloway, Cathy Urwin, Conze Venn and Valerie Walkerdine (eds), *Changing the Subject: Psychology, Social Regulation and Subjectivity*, London: Methuen, 228–52.

Hoodfar, Homa 1988: 'Household budgeting and financial management in a lower-income Cairo neighbourhood'. In Daisy Dwyer and Judith Bruce (eds), *A Home Divided*, Stanford: Stanford University Press, 120–42.

hooks, bell 1984: *Feminist Theory from Margin to Center*. Boston: South End Press.

hooks, bell 1991: *Yearning: Race, Gender and Cultural Politics*. London: Turnaround Press.

Humphrey, Caroline 1974: 'Inside a Mongolian tent'. *New Society*, October: 21–8.

Humphries, Jane 1979: 'Class struggle and the persistence of the working class family'. *Cambridge Journal of Economics*, 1 (3): 241–58.

Irigaray, Luce 1985: *This Sex Which Is Not One*. Ithaca: Cornell University Press.

Jackson, Michael 1983: 'Knowledge of the body'. *Man*, 18 (2): 327–45.

Jones, Christine 1983: 'The mobilisation of women's labor for cash crop production: a game theoretic-approach'. *American Journal of Agricultural Economics*, 65: 1049–54.

Jones, Christine 1986: 'Intra-household bargaining in response to the introduction of new crops: a case study from north Cameroon'. In Joyce Moock (ed.), *Understanding Africa's Rural Households and Farming Systems*, Boulder, Colo.: Westview Press, 105–23.

Kabbani, Rana 1986: *Europe's Myths of Orient*. London: Macmillan.

Kapferer, Bruce 1988: 'The anthropologist as hero: three exponents of postmodernist anthropology'. *Critiques of Anthropology*, 8 (2): 77–104.

Kirby, Vicki 1989: 'Re-writing: postmodernism and ethnography'. *Mankind*, 19 (1): 36–45.

Kirby, Vicki 1991: 'Comment on Mascia-Lees, Sharpe and Cohen's "The postmodernist turn in anthropology: cautions from a feminist perspective"'. *Signs*, 16 (2): 394–400.

Kirby, Vicki 1993: 'Feminisms and postmodernisms: anthropology and the management of difference'. *Anthropological Quarterly*, 66 (3): 127–33.

Kristeva, Julia 1980: *Desire in Language*. New York: Columbia University Press.

Kuper, Adam 1973: *Anthropologists and Anthropology: The British School 1922–1972*. London: Allen Lane.

Lacan, Jacques 1977: *Écrits: A Selection*. London: Tavistock.

Laqueur, Thomas 1990: *Making Sex: Body and Gender from the Greeks to Freud*. Cambridge, Mass.: Harvard University Press.

Lazareg, Marina 1988: 'Feminism and difference: The perils of writing as a woman on women in Algeria'. *Feminist Issues*, 14 (1): 81–107.

Leenhardt, Maurice [1947] 1979: *Do Kamo: Person and Myth in the Melanesian World*. Chicago: University of Chicago Press.

Levi-Strauss, Claude 1969: *The Elementary Structures of Kinship*. Boston: Beacon Press.

Lienhardt, Godfrey 1985: 'Self: public, private. Some African representations'. In Michael Carrithers, Steven Collins and Steven Lukes (eds), *The Category of the Person*, Cambridge: Cambridge University Press, 141–55.

Lutz, Catherine 1988: *Unnatural Emotions: Everyday Sentiments on a Micronesian Atoll and Their Challenge to Western Theory*. Chicago: University of Chicago Press.

Lutz, Catherine 1990: 'The erasure of women's writing in sociocultural anthropology'. *American Ethnologist*, 17 (4): 611–27.

Lutz, Catherine and Abu-Lughod, Lila (eds) 1990: *Language and the Politics of Emotion*. Cambridge: Cambridge University Press.

MacCormack, Carol and Strathern, Marilyn (eds) 1980: *Nature, Culture and Gender*. Cambridge: Cambridge University Press.

McHugh, Ernestine L. 1989: 'Concepts of the person among the Gurungs of Nepal'. *American Ethnologist*, 16 (1): 75–86.

Mackintosh, Maureen 1979: 'Domestic labour and the household'. In Sandra Burman (ed.), *Fit Work for Women*, London: Croom Helm.

McNay, Lois 1992: *Foucault and Feminism*. Cambridge: Polity Press.

Mahoney, Maureen and Yngvesson, Barbara 1992: 'The construction of subjectivity and the paradox of resistance: reintegrating feminist anthropology and psychology'. *Signs*, 18 (1): 44–73.

Margolis, Diane 1989: 'Considering women's experience: a reformulation of power theory'. *Theory and Society*, 18: 387–416.

Marks, Elaine and de Courtivron, Isabelle 1981: *New French Feminisms*. London: Harvester Press.

Marriott, Kim 1976: 'Hindu transactions: diversity without duration'. In Bruce Kapferer (ed.), *Transactions and Meanings*, Philadelphia: Institute for the Study of Human Values.

Mascia-Lees, Frances, Sharpe, Patricia and Cohen, Collen Ballerino 1989: 'The postmodernist turn in anthropology: cautions from a feminist perspective'. *Signs*, 15 (1): 7–33.

Mascia-Lees, Frances, Sharpe, Patricia and Cohen, Collen Ballerino 1991: Reply to Kirby. *Signs*, 16 (2): 401–8.

Mead, G. H. 1934: *Mind, Self and Society*. Chicago: University of Chicago Press.

Meigs, Anna 1990: 'Multiple gender ideologies and statuses'. In Peggy Reeves Sanday and Ruth Goodenough (eds), *Beyond the Second Sex: New Directions in the Anthropology of Gender*, Philadelphia: University of Pennsylvania Press, 101–12.

Meillassoux, Claude 1981: *Maidens, Meal and Money*. Cambridge: Cambridge University Press.

Miller, Nancy 1991: *Getting Personal*. London: Routledge.

Minh-ha, Trinh 1989: *Woman, Native, Other: Writing, Post-coloniality and Feminism*. Bloomington: Indiana University Press.

Minh-ha, Trinh 1991: *When the Moon Waxes Red: Representation, Gender and Cultural Politics*. London: Routledge.

Mitchell, Juliet 1974: *Psychoanalysis and Feminism*. Harmondsworth: Penguin.

Mitchell, Juliet and Rose, Jacqueline 1982: *Feminine Sexuality: Jacques Lacan and the École Freudienne*. London: Macmillan.

Mohanty, Chandra 1991: 'Under western eyes: feminist scholarship and colonial discourses'. In Chandra Mohanty, Ann Russo and Lourdes Torres (eds), *Third World Women and the Politics of Feminism*, Bloomington: Indiana University Press, 51–80.

Moore, Henrietta L. 1986: *Space, Text and Gender: An Anthropological Study of the Marakwet of Kenya*. Cambridge: Cambridge University Press.

Moore, Henrietta L. 1988: *Feminism and Anthropology*. Cambridge: Polity Press.

Moore, Henrietta L. 1990a: 'Paul Ricoeur: action, meaning and text'. In Christopher Tilley (ed.), *Reading Material Culture*, Oxford: Basil Blackwell, 85–120.

Moore, Henrietta L. 1990b: 'Visions of the good life: anthropology and the study of utopias'. *Cambridge Anthropology*, 14 (3): 13–33.

Moore, Henrietta L. 1993a: 'The differences within and the differences between'. In Teresa del Valle (ed.), *Gendered Anthropology*, London: Routledge, 193–204.

Moore, Henrietta L. 1993b: 'Gender and the modelling of the economy.' In Sutti Ortiz and Susan Lees (eds), *Understanding Economic Process*, Lanham: University Press of America, 131–48.

Morgan, Robyn 1988: *The Demon Lover: On the Sexuality of Terrorism*. New York: W. W. Norton.

Morrison, Toni 1992: *Playing in the Dark*. Harvard: Harvard University Press.

Obeyesekere, Gananath 1981: *Medusa's Hair: An Essay on Personal Symbols and Religious Experience*. Chicago: University of Chicago Press.

Ortner, Sherry 1974: 'Is female to male as nature is to culture?' In Michelle Rosaldo and Louise Lamphere (eds), *Woman, Culture and Society*, Stanford: Stanford University Press, 67–88.

Ortner, Sherry and Whitehead, Harriet (eds) 1981: *Sexual Meanings: The Cultural Construction of Gender and Sexuality*. Cambridge: Cambridge University Press.

Pahl, Jan 1989: *Money and Marriage*. Basingstoke: Macmillan Education.

Pratt, Mary Louise 1986: 'Fieldwork in common places'. In James Clifford and George Marcus (eds), *Writing Culture: The Poetics and Politics of Ethnography*, Berkeley: University of California Press, 27–50.

Pratt, Mary Louise 1992: *Imperial Eyes: Travel Writing and Transculturation*. London: Routledge.

Pred, Allan 1990: *Making Histories and Constructing Human Geographies*. Boulder, Colo.: Westview Press.

Probyn, Elspeth 1993: *Sexing the Self: Gendered Positions in Cultural Studies*. London: Routledge.

Ragland-Sullivan, Ellie 1986: *Jacques Lacan and the Philosophy of Psychoanalysis*. Urbana: University of Illinois Press.

Rich, Adrienne 1976: *Of Woman Born*. New York: W. W. Norton.

Rich, Adrienne 1986: 'Notes towards a politics of location'. In *Blood, Bread and Poetry: Selected Prose, 1979–1985*, New York: W. W. Norton.

Riley, Denise 1988: *'Am I That Name?': Feminism and the Category of 'Women' in History*. London: Macmillan.

Robertson, A. F. 1991: *Beyond the Family*. Cambridge: Polity Press.

Roland, Alan 1988: *In Search of Self: Toward a Cross-cultural Psychology*. Princeton: Princeton University Press.

Roldan, Martha 1988: 'Renegotiating the marital contract: intrahousehold patterns of money allocation and women's subordination among domestic outworkers in Mexico City'. In Daisy Dwyer and Judith Bruce (eds), *A Home Divided*, Stanford: Stanford University Press, 229–47.

Rosaldo, Michelle 1974: 'Woman, culture and society: a theoretical overview'. In Michellel Rosaldo and Louise Lamphere (eds), *Woman, Culture and Society*, Stanford: Stanford University Press, 17–42.

Rosaldo, Michelle 1980: 'The use and abuse of anthropology: reflections on feminism and cross-cultural understanding'. *Signs*, 5 (3): 389–417.

Roscoe, Will 1988: 'We'Wha and Klah: the American Indian Berdache as artist and priest'. *American Indian Quarterly*, 12 (2): 127–50.

Rose, Jacqueline 1983: 'Femininity and its discontents'. *Feminist Review*, 14: 5–21.

Rose, Jacqueline 1986: *Sexuality in the Field of Vision*. London: Verso.

Sacks, Karen 1989: 'Toward a unified theory of class, race and gender'. *American Ethnologist*, 16 (3): 534–50.

Sage, Lorna 1992: *Women in the House of Fiction: Post-war Women Novelists*. London: Macmillan.

Sahlins, Marshall 1974: *Stone Age Economics*. Chicago: Chicago University Press.

Sanday, Peggy Reeves and Goodenough, Ruth (eds) 1990: *Beyond the Second Sex: New Directions in the Anthropology of Gender*. Philadelphia: University of Pennsylvania Press.

Schor, Naomi 1989: 'This essentialism which is not one: coming to grips with Irigaray'. *Differences*, 1 (2): 38–58.

Scott, James 1985: *Weapons of the Weak: Everyday Forms of Peasant Resistance*. New Haven: Yale University Press.

Shweder, Richard 1991: *Thinking through Cultures: Expeditions in Cultural Psychology*. Cambridge, Mass.: Harvard University Press.

Silverman, Kaja 1988: *The Acoustic Mirror*. Bloomington: Indiana University Press.

Smith, Jean 1981: 'Self and experience in Maori culture'. In Paul Heelas and Andrew Lock (eds), *Indigenous Psychologies: The Anthropology of the Self*, London: Academic Press.

Smith, Paul 1988: *Discerning the Subject*. Minnesota: University of Minnesota Press.

Soja, Edward 1989: *Postmodern Geographies: The Reassertion of Space in Critical Social Theory*. London: Verso.

Sommer, Doris 1988: 'Not just a personal story: women's testimonios and the plural self'. In B. Brodzki and C. Schenck (eds), *Life/Lines: Theorising Women's Autobiography*, Ithaca: Cornell University Press, 107–30.

Spivak, Gayatri Chakravorty 1992: 'French feminism revisited: ethics and politics'. In Judith Butler and Joan Scott (eds), *Feminists Theorise the Political*, London: Routledge.

Stanton, Domna 1986: 'Difference on trial: a critique of the maternal metaphor in Kristeva and Irigaray'. In Nancy Miller (ed.), *The Poetics of Gender*, New York: Columbia University Press, 157–82.

Stocking, George 1983: 'The ethnographer's magic: fieldwork in British anthropology from Tylor to Malinowski'. In George Stocking (ed.), *Observers Observed: Essays on Ethnographic Fieldwork*, Madison: University of Wisconsin Press, 70–121.

Stoler, Ann 1989: 'Making empire respectable: the politics of race and sexual morality in 20th century colonial cultures'. *American Ethnologist*, 16 (4): 634–60.

Stoler, Ann 1991: 'Carnal knowledge and imperial power: gender, race and morality in colonial Asia'. In M. di Leonardo (ed.), *Gender at the Crossroads of Knowledge*, Berkeley: University of California Press, 51–102.

Strathern, Marilyn 1984: 'Domesticity and the denigration of women'. In Denise O'Brien and Sharon Tiffany (eds), *Rethinking Women's Roles: Perspectives from the Pacific*, Berkeley: University of California Press, 13–31.

Strathern, Marilyn 1987: *Understanding Inequality*. Cambridge: Cambridge University Press.

Strathern, Marilyn 1988: *The Gender of the Gift*. Berkeley: University of California Press.

Strauss, Anne 1982: 'The structure of the self in Northern Cheyenne culture'. In Benjamin Lee (ed.), *Psychosocial Theories of the Self*, New York: Plenum Press.

Suleiman, Susan 1986: *The Female Body in Western Culture*. Cambridge, Mass.: Harvard University Press.

Taussig, Michael 1986: *Shamanism, Colonialism and the Wild Man: A Study in Terror and Healing*. Chicago: University of Chicago Press.

Taylor, Barbara 1983: *Eve and the New Jerusalem: Socialism and Feminism in the Nineteenth Century*. London: Virago.

Thomas, Nicholas 1994: *Colonialism's Culture*. Cambridge: Polity Press.

Thornton, Robert 1983: 'Narrative ethnography in Africa, 1850–1920: the creation and capture of an appropriate domain for anthropology'. *Man*, 18: 502–20.

Tilley, Christopher (ed.) 1990: *Reading Material Culture*. Oxford: Basil Blackwell.

Torgovnick, Marianna 1990: *Gone Primitive: Savage Intellects, Modern Lives*. Chicago: University of Chicago Press.

Tress, Daryl McGowan 1988: 'Comment on Flax's "Postmodernism and gender relations in feminist theory"'. *Signs*, 14 (1): 196–203.

Vaughan, Megan 1991: *Curing Their Ills*. Cambridge: Polity Press.

Wade, Peter 1994: 'Man the Hunter: Gender and Violence in music and drinking contexts in Colombia'. In Peter Gow and Penelope Harvey (eds) *Sex and Violence: Issues in Representation and Experience*. London: Routledge.

Wagner, Roy 1975: *The Invention of Culture*. Englewood Cliffs, NJ: Prentice-Hall.

Weedon, Chris 1987: *Feminist Practice and Poststructuralist Theory*. Oxford: Basil Blackwell.

Whitehead, Ann 1981: 'I'm hungry Mum: the politics of domestic budgeting'. In Kate Young, Carol Wolkowitz and Roslyn McCullagh (eds), *Of Marriage and the Market*, London: CSE Books, 88–111.

Whitehead, Ann 1984: 'Beyond the household: gender and kinship based resource allocation in a Ghanaian domestic economy'. Unpublished paper presented at workshop on Conceptualing the Household, Harvard University.

Whitehead, Harriet 1981: 'The bow and the burden strap: a new look at institutionalised homosexuality in native North America'. In Sherry Ortner and Harriet Whitehead (eds), *Sexual Meanings: The Cultural Construction of Gender and Sexuality*, Cambridge: Cambridge University Press, 80–115.

Whittaker, Elvi 1992: 'The birth of the anthropological self and its career'. *Ethos*, 20 (2): 191–219.

Williams, Drid 1975: 'The brides of Christ'. In Shirley Ardener (ed.), *Perceiving Women*, London: J. M. Dent, 105–26.

Williams, W. 1986: *The Spirit and the Flesh: Sexual Diversity in American Indian Culture*. Boston: Beacon Press.

Yanagisako, Sylvia and Collier, Jane 1987: 'Toward a unified analysis of gender and kinship'. In Jane Collier and Sylvia Yanagisako (eds), *Gender and Kinship: Essays toward a Unified Analysis*, Stanford: Stanford University Press, 14–50.

INDEX